From Adolescence to Zenobia

To Tammie + Scott,
whom our journeys continue —
to be pretty amazing.
love,

From Adolescence to Zenobia

true stories of the human element

in the journey through school

by Stephen Fuller

TATE PUBLISHING & Enterprises

Published by Tate Publishing & Enterprises, LLC
127 E. Trade Center Terrace | Mustang, Oklahoma 73064 USA
1.888.361.9473 | www.tatepublishing.com

Tate Publishing is committed to excellence in the publishing industry. The company reflects the philosophy established by the founders, based on Psalm 68:11,
"The Lord gave the word and great was the company of those who published it."

Book design copyright © 2008 by Tate Publishing, LLC. All rights reserved.
Cover design & Interior Design by Janae J. Glass

Published in the United States of America

ISBN: 978-1-60696-653-2
1. Biography & Autobiography: Educators
2. General Interest: General Topics: Humor

08.10.24

Dedication

To my wife, Janice, who has always put others before herself, including me and my chosen career, which sometimes interfered with her own choice–being an exemplary mother to our three sons. She nevertheless accomplished her goal and supported me in mine to the extent that, without her, these stories would never have happened.

Acknowledgements

I would like to thank my parents, my teachers, my coaches, and my friends and colleagues, all of whom instilled in me the importance of education, not as preparation for living in some other time and place, but as a time and place to live.

Table of Contents

Introduction

I decided to write this book of stories because, over the course of my thirty-six years in education, every time I would tell one of them, my friends would tell me I should write a book.

"You should write a book of these stories," they would say (I did not say my friends were very original). "I bet you have a million of them."

Well, I do not have a million, but pretty close to it. I have enjoyed recording them here, if for no other reason than the cathartic effect I experience after I get them down on paper. I hope also that they have some benefit for the reader.

For me, soon after becoming an administrator, it was both beneficial and humbling to find out the truth about the way the kids saw me, the disciplinarian in the school. One day, I was chastising a quick-thinking seventh grader named Jim for a major transgression. When he denied having done anything wrong, I asked him why then, when he had seen me coming, he had so quickly run the other way. Jim looked at me, then over each shoulder, then leaned forward and said, "Well have you looked around? You're not exactly the school mascot, you know!"

It was about then that I began to see the humor and the

lessons occurring all around me in this job. I learned over the years to appreciate the humor, share it with others, and be ready for the invaluable lesson that would come right behind it. I am living proof that much of the learning done in schools is done by people other than the ones labeled "student."

What I have learned from these stories and many others has been invaluable to me as a person. It has also proven to me something that I think I always knew, but now can see more clearly. School is not preparation for life; school *is* life. These kids, I came to realize, have been living life to the fullest. That desperate, all-out quest to find out who they are and to become that person is what makes this book worth reading.

The first story is one of the shortest and is different because it is about me as a student, but after you read it, you will see the important role a good start in school plays in the life of any child and the role a parent never escapes, no matter what age her "child" is. A couple of the other stories are also about my own experiences as a student, and one is not even about school at all, but you will see why it is included as a "lesson."

After that first story, you begin the journey from "Adolescence" to "Zenobia," something that will become clear to you as you read. As you take this journey, be aware that the objective is just that—a journey—not a destination.

A friend and I were planning a workshop for teachers years ago. She said the story I had picked out to illustrate a certain point might not relate. We thought about it and then decided, "If it's a good story, everything relates."

I really believe that. If a story touches us in some way, it can spawn endless individual lessons for us all. That is what this collection of stories is about. Read them and write your own lesson, or just read them and *enjoy*.

One more thing: much is written and taught to educators these days about the technical side of the profession. Are you teaching what will be on the test, using the recognized best practices, observing the correct benchmarks, and so forth? But what is being left out too often is the human element. What are you doing here? Who are your kids? How do they feel? How can you make their lives better? Since I began in this business in 1972 until now, those things have not changed, and I suspect they never will. That is why you should take this book, sit in a school desk somewhere, and not just read it, but also, at least in your mind, *live* it.

Stephen W. Fuller

The Green Pencil Shirt

It was the first day of the first grade in 1955, my first day of any kind of school, and I was a little bit scared. To bolster my confidence, however, I had my brand new box of fat Crayola Crayons, my Big Chief Writing Tablet, and my fat red pencil. Mother took me into the room and I started to feel better because I really was excited about going to school. But mostly, I was confident because of my brand new green pencil shirt. Mother had taken me to Montgomery Wards to buy the material and then had proceeded to make something wearable out of the bolt of cloth. My first day turned out to be just fine and school became a good place for me, even providing for me a career in education.

April 2005 and Mother lay on her deathbed, just a few days short of her 80th birthday. I made the two-hundred-mile trip to see her one last time. Although it was hard to speak, in that conversation she said some remarkable things, not the least of which was that she had a boat with her name on it that was coming to take her away. She said, "Isn't that nice?"

On the way there, I had tried to come up with a way to approach the subject of what we both knew was happening. Now, since she had brought it up, I had an opening. I said,

"Mother, do you remember my first day of school? You took me to the room and stood at the back with the other mothers. I had my new box of Crayolas, my writing tablet, and my pencil, but I was most proud of my new shirt you made me–green with pencils on it, remember?"

She smiled and nodded, very weak.

"I remember thinking how much fun school was going to be, and looking back at you smiling. Then after a while, I got so distracted that I did not look back as often. When I did, I remember the feeling I had when I saw you and the other mothers had left! I thought, 'we really are going to do this.'"

She was just smiling, remembering.

"Mother," I said, "This feels kind of like that. I saw that you were gone, but it was okay, because you had done your job and gotten me where I was supposed to be—on my own. Now, it's the same thing. We will look back and you will be gone, but we will be okay, because you did your job; you got us where we should be—on our own. You did a good job."

Mother smiled and with difficulty said, "My, my, I guess we really are going to do this."

Mother died two days later, without being able to talk to me anymore. I keep that conversation as one of my most treasured memories. A few weeks later, however, two more treasures appeared.

When we four brothers got together with our wives to divide up several personal things, we said a prayer and started choosing from oldest to youngest and back again, with amazingly no real disagreement on what would go to whom. There were about 20 oil paintings in the house that Mother had done since joining an art class soon after our father had died. She had loved to paint. There were all kinds, but most were idyllic country scenes. One painting that caught my eye, however, I had never noticed before. As I looked closer and remembered that precious conversation on Mother's deathbed, I had to have it. "I want *this* one," I said when it was my turn. I held up the twelve-by-eighteen-inch, framed picture in disbelief. The scene was a darkening sky over a river (was it dawn or dusk?), with a canoe in the foreground, empty and resting against the bank. Next to the bow, in the lower right-hand corner of the painting, she had signed her name, as was her custom. As I read, "Mildred Fuller" on the canvas, I began to choke. "The boat with her name on it!" I said. That picture hangs in my office today.

But the real treasure came a few days later as we continued cleaning out Mother's house. My nephew handed down a sealed box from the attic to me, which I gave to my wife, Janice. As I walked away from her, she screamed. "Steve! Look!" There it was, in a plastic bag, lying right on top of other clothes in the dusty cardboard container–the green pencil shirt! Tears streaming down her face, she held up this little garment from my past, Mother's gift to my confidence on my first day of school, and her lasting contribution to my life.

Today, the green pencil shirt is encased, along with an abbreviated version of this story, in a frame in our kitchen. At parties, I have seen many a person, coffee and cookie in hand, stop to read and reflect on it. To the old, it may be calling up their own memories of their first day; to the younger readers, maybe their own role as a new parent. Whatever the case, I hope it serves as a reminder that when it is the first day of school, that all-important beginning of life—not just preparation for it—doing something special for your child is a wonderfully symbolic way to start their education. I hope whatever it is a parent chooses it lasts for 50 years—like my shirt—and beyond.

Martha and the "A"

Martha was a worrywart. Soon after arriving in the seventh grade at our junior high school, she discovered the nurse, who was next door to the office I occupied as one of the guidance counselors in our school. My location made me privy to a world of conversations about the frailties of the human body that I had previously thought impossible.

On Monday, Martha had a stomach virus. On Tuesday, a headache. So on it went until Friday ended with some kind of unexplainable ache in her arm or a stiff ankle joint. Sometimes her vision was affected. Other times, she could not hear well. The nurse practiced her best "patient patience," but Martha was not to be denied. There was something wrong with her, she was sure. To all of the nurse's diagnostic questions, she gave what she thought would be the answer most likely to confirm what she thought she knew—that she was dying. She even forced the nurse to play her trump card for malingerers ("Do your teeth itch?") that nurses sometimes use to discern truth from medical fiction. All of this, of course, was affecting her productivity in the classroom. Her grades began to suffer. This brought her young, inexperienced, busy mother reluctantly into the picture.

Although it was evident to most of us at school what was going on, Mom could not see it. We all knew that what was really causing the academic problems was probably the amount of time spent out of the classroom in pursuit of the latest ailment and its "cure," rather than any physical shortcoming itself. The more Martha was able to con the teachers into letting her go to the nurse in the first place (she was a very convincing charmer), the more she was able to go home and convince Mom that there was really something dreadfully wrong with her. This, in spite of the fact that the nurse always told her the same thing: "Martha, I really can't find anything wrong. Go back to class."

If you have ever worked in a school or been a parent, you are ahead of me. You can see what was coming—the dreaded *team conference*. Sure enough, the date was set, the parent was notified, and we were all there. It was decided, along with the usual reminders about assignment notebooks, after-school tutoring, and the like that maybe Martha's mother should take her to the doctor to have her checked out, once and for all. Even to Mom, whose attention we all suspected was the real target of Martha's manipulations, the list of daily maladies was beginning to defy the odds.

So, the appointment was made and in the not-too-distant future (thank God) the time would come when Martha would have her answer. Would it be cancer, heart trouble, typhoid, arthritis, maybe a rare form of congenital hangnail? In the interim between the conference and the appointment, Martha consumed herself with these questions. She came by every day with a new theory. The nurse and I had the same questions, and began to pray for a cancellation of someone's appointment so the doctor could see her sooner.

Finally, the day came. She went in the afternoon and did not come back to school that day. The secretary's typewriter hummed again, the nurse actually saw someone else, and I got back to changing schedules and listening to kids with worse problems than hypochondria. It was a welcome break from our routine of listening to Martha's laundry list of liabilities.

The next day, bright and early, Martha bounded into the nurse's office with the news. "I found out," she said. "I found out what's wrong with me!" She went into the office with the nurse, who looked at me as if to say, "She must have gotten to the doctor, too."

A few minutes later, a happy, bouncing Martha came out and went to class. The nurse was shaking her head.

"Well, what is it?" we all asked breathlessly.

"I don't know," she answered. "She said he told her she had a condition that was treatable, and that she shouldn't worry too much about it. It was something she had never heard of. Unfortunately, she couldn't remember the name of it. She said she thinks it starts with an 'A.'"

For the rest of the day, since we could not reach the parent by phone, we racked our brains in search of the condition that might explain the doctor's diagnosis. The nurse even searched the entire "A" section of the *Physician's Desktop Reference* (the school nurse's "Bible"), but to no avail. Whatever this was may be treatable, but it was certainly *rare*.

Fortunately, at the end of the day, Martha came skipping in again.

"I remembered, I remembered!" she announced to all. "I remembered that my mom wrote down the name of the disease I have on this piece of paper for me. She handed a crumpled slip to the nurse. With a suppressed grin showing on her face, the nurse read the name to the rest of us. "Adolescence."

I don't know where Martha went or whatever became of her, but I am pretty sure of one thing. Whether she ever found a cure for her "ailment" or not, barring any accident or bona fide serious illness, I bet she outgrew it.

The "National Middle School" & Other Interview Questions

To ensure that we are helping kids on their journey through adolescence, there are certain things we have to get right, but one of the things we educators do the poorest job of is choosing more of us.

That is not to say that we are always hiring the wrong people, it's just that we often go about it in the most boring, mundane, pointless ways. I have seen some interviews, from both sides of the desk, that could be used to cure insomnia. They just keep droning on and on about things we think are important: hypothetical situations, philosophies of education (gag!), and the like. I decided after a few years of trying to get a thirty-minute snapshot of a person I might spend the next ten years working with, that I was doing it all wrong.

First, I firmly believe that there is no canned set of interview questions that can get to the meat of what you want to know. People have written many such things and applied all kinds of formulas, matrices, spreadsheets, ranking sheets, all trying to quantify what cannot be measured mathematically.

Second, if that is true, then why waste time on such questions? What you really want to know is two things: can this person teach and can I work with him/her? You should be able to get the rest from a résumé, application, or transcript, or from talking to references, all of which I recommend.

So if not "Please tell me your philosophy of education," then what do you ask? I developed a way of interviewing teachers that I think worked better. At least it never put anybody to sleep.

The first question I would usually ask was derived from a conversation years ago with my older brother. David, the oldest, is a successful high school football coach who said something that stuck with me.

The statement was made sort of tongue-in-cheek because his own son was in middle school at the time, but if it had been true it would have been a remarkable comment on the care and feeding of middle schoolers. As we talked at a family gathering about school things (about which we often disagreed), he said something like "I have no use for middle school kids. As far as I'm concerned, there should be a national middle school and they should have it in *Montana* or somewhere. Just send them back when they're ready for high school!" Such was his frustration with the middle school mind. We laughed about that, but then I decided later it would make a good introductory interview question.

Eventually, I came to use that quote at the start of every teacher interview. In thinking about my own family, I remembered how relentlessly my younger brother Paul, had teased Joel, the youngest, when Joel was about twelve. Paul was about seventeen and could not understand why Joel was so clumsy, awkward, uncool, poorly dressed, just plain goofy. In fact, he nicknamed him "Stone Goofy," or "S.G." for short.

In Joel's defense, his early adolescence was not worse than ours and he did grow out of it, but I realized now that here I was, working with all these twelve to fourteen year olds, and that was what was wrong with them–they were just "Stone Goofy." Then it occurred to me, *I want teachers who can see that.*

So I started my interviews with David's comment and asked this question: "Why would anybody have such a low opinion of middle school kids?" If they did not laugh when they heard his assessment of middle schoolers, they could not answer that question satisfactorily, so I did not hire them. It worked beautifully for me.

The point is, get people discussing something about which they can be passionate. The good ones came back at me after that first question with their own experiences with middle schoolers. The others sometimes looked at me with blank stares and said things like, "I have no idea, I really like the kids," or some other bogus, kiss-up answer they thought I wanted to hear.

If I could use that kind of question, I then thought, why not do the whole interview that way? After all, I wanted to see what people thought, not what they could regurgitate from some education class at the university. So I used quotes for almost every topic. Sometimes the quotes were things I made up. Sometimes they were truisms I had always heard but could not give the source, and once in a while they were from some other author. The list looked something like this:

> (*On behavior*) Here is a quote from me. "The fastest growing part of a middle schooler's body is his mouth."
> What does that mean to you?

(*On socialization*) Again from me. "The thing I have noticed about middle school kids is that, if they don't get involved in something, they will get involved in something." What does that mean to you?

(*Discipline*) Lee Canter says you should do three things: tell them what you want, tell them what you will do if you don't get it, and then if you don't get it, do it. Tell me how you do that.

(*Lesson plans*) It is said that every good lesson has a place where you tell them what you are going to tell them, you tell them, and then you tell them what you told them. How do you make sure that happens in your lesson plans?

(*Parents*) Some of our parents are what I call, "double-income, double-degree, and double-SUV." They have everything they want and their child is on a path to Harvard, the NBA, or Hollywood and you are just a little speedbump along the way. How do you deal with someone like that?

(*Special Education*) There is sometimes an issue of fairness for regular education teachers dealing with Special Education laws and regulations. We operate under the assumption that "fair is not everybody getting the same thing. Fair is everybody getting what they need." What does that mean to you?

(*Support from the administration*) When there is a conflict between teacher and student or teacher and parent or all three, we operate under the basic assumption that "the teacher is always right—unless the teacher is wrong."

What does that mean to you? (This one usually raises
an eyebrow because it sounds so nonsensical, until they
realize that what is important is that they are respected as
the adult, paid professional in the room, but they have an
obligation to be right or admit when they are not.)

Sometimes I would end with a quote that had nothing to do
with the educational system, such as one from Mark Twain
that I used: "We must all endeavor to live our lives in such a
way that when we die, even the undertaker is sorry." I would
ask them to expand that thought, so I could see, again, if they
were able to be passionate about something they believed.
A young 22-year-old was given that quote one time and
she looked at me with a pale, blank stare that let me know
she did not understand. I thought she had blown it, but she
leaned over and said, "Undertaker?" She did not understand
the word. When I said, "You know, funeral home director, a
mortician." She straightened up and said, "Oh, yes! I can tell
you about that. My father just died and I know he lived that
kind of life." And she went on to give me a beautiful answer—
just what I wanted.

My track record with interviewing was as good as or better than anyone else's in my district and our turnover rate was
consistently the lowest. I think these questions had something to do with that. At least I know they made it much
more fun.

There were some other memorable interviews, too, like
the two I did over the phone without ever meeting the appli-
cant in person. Or the woman who was so arrogant that she
tried to interview me and indicated that if I didn't change
certain things, she would not be interested. Then there was

the interview I let go on a little too long one late afternoon and it ended up making me late to leave the building to avoid an approaching tornado, which I rode out in the vault.

The most unusual interview, however, had to be the one I did for a bookkeeper a few years ago. The man's résumé looked really good, maybe too good, but I was always diversifying my staff and another male in the office might be a good move. During the interview, the man had a *seizure*. He was about to answer a question when he turned his head at a funny angle, screwed up his eyebrows, twisted his mouth as if about to say something, but just stayed that way. In a few seconds, I recognized it and went to get the nurse. We talked him down as it went away and his wife, who was waiting in the car, came in sighing about how often this had happened, about how he just could not have done the job, even if he had been hired.

Interviews are perhaps the most artificial times in our lives in many ways, but I learned over the years that they do not have to be. If you can just get a person to talk–meaningfully, humorously, passionately–about something you hope they will love, you have uncovered their philosophy of education without ever having to be bored to tears by it and you will have found someone worth keeping.

Stan's Planet

It took a lot of special people to help Stan on his journey, which could sometimes be described as somewhat "extraterrestrial." Stan was a big kid who always seemed a little "different" to most people. He was in the seventh grade, but his social maturity, or lack of it, defied grade levels. He was in a world of his own. That was why most of his peers, and some of his teachers, described him regularly as being "from another planet."

To be sure, with his extreme size, his blond hair combed straight forward and nearly reaching his eyes, his odd mannerisms, and his distinctive, almost silly voice, Stan stood out at school. Diagnosed as emotionally disturbed, Stan was receiving the best education he could in this large public middle school. He had special classes for learning social skills, while being included as much as possible, as the law mandates, in regular academic classes with his peers.

That was the problem. Who were his peers? He did not seem to have any because he was so bizarre. Students and staff members reported regularly seeing him walk up and down the streets of the neighborhood, talking aloud to the voices he said he heard from "the people from outer space."

In school, if the class were reading something individually, many teachers might decide to let the students choose their own locations for that activity. Some would be at their desks, some seated on the floor, some reclining on a table, or some on large pillows kept in the room just for this purpose. Stan was the kind of kid who would ignore that kind of freedom when it was reading time, but opt to sit under a table in the fetal position during a test, when everyone else was required to be in their desks. During this time, he might babble on about outer space or blurt out silly, irrelevant remarks that often made his teachers angry and might result in his being sent out of the room.

On one of these occasions, I had my first serious encounter with Stan. I was the principal of the school and, although I had two assistant principals who usually handled the discipline referrals, on this particular day they were not available, so he was sent to me. Stan's reputation for weirdness had preceded him, so already I expected there would be trouble communicating. I had actually only talked to the boy directly once before, and the circumstances of that meeting were on my mind as he sat in my office that day.

That first meeting had been on a warm, muggy, Texas morning in August of his first year with us, when I was on my way to school. It was during the first week of school and the temperature, even at 7:45 a.m., was a soggy 85 degrees, sure to go close to 100 before the end of the day. As I stopped at the intersection right in front of the school and waited for some students to cross in the normal crosswalk manner, I saw something very peculiar. A tall boy was walking across in heavy traffic on this already hot day wearing a parka; hood pulled up and tied tight around his chin, and heavy gloves. He walked with both arms extended fully at right angles, airplane-style. What's more, he was crossing the street *diagonally*, right through the center of the busy intersection!

I turned the corner and headed into the parking lot, turning my head to keep the boy in view as he made his way up to the front of the school. I waited for him near the door. Other kids were busy as they waited for the first bell, playing soccer with a crushed can, or chasing girls around the bike rack, or trading baseball cards, and all were wearing the typical "uniform" of the season—shorts and a t-shirt. The parka-zipped Stan approached the school, to my amazement, without raising one adolescent eyebrow in the crowd near the door. His classmates, it seemed, had come to expect the unusual from Stan. They literally gave him his "space."

I asked Stan his name, he told me, and without that information meaning much to me yet, I proceeded to give him a safety lecture on the inadvisability of crossing an intersection diagonally, and so on. He listened blankly and then I asked about his garb. He offered no plausible excuse for wearing the parka, mumbled something about liking it, and seemed to wonder what his crime might have been. I wondered the same as far as the coat was concerned. There is no law against being different, I reminded myself. I let it go and he lumbered away toward an empty spot on the playground.

I had come away from that encounter with an appreciation for Stan's ability to be bizarre, and now, with him sitting in my office over a year later, I was remembering the other little things I had heard from his teachers that seemed to suggest some kind of "other-worldliness" about him. They saw him alternately as a disruptive force in the classroom, and a classic, pathetic figure to be comforted. Still, his bizarre social interaction made it impossible for even his most sensitive teachers to get very close to him.

Now, sitting in my office, he was accused of making strange noises during the lesson, saying inappropriate things to other students near him, insisting on sitting under a table, rolling on the floor, and otherwise distracting students when the teacher desperately needed everyone's attention at the front of the room. He had been babbling about spacemen and other planets until the teacher had given up and sent him to me. Confronting Stan with his behavior, normally the first step I would take in such an encounter with other miscreants, quickly proved futile. He did not even seem to acknowledge the behavior itself, let alone its impropriety. We talked in parallel conversation, me about his behavior and he about people who don't understand, about solutions to problems that might come from outer space, and about voices he heard, and so forth.

I must admit to copping out and resorting to the usual consequences for his behavior (detention, in-school suspension, behavior essays) for lack of better alternatives. I did refer him though, to the school counselor and to the school psychologist for counseling, and I called his mother. Of course, these interventions had been tried many times before, with little difference being made. In addition to her sad, weary voice, I also felt I could hear his mother's head shaking over the phone. She did not know any better than the rest of us what to do for her son.

So it was that Stan dug deeper into his comfort zone,

which to us seemed more like the Twilight Zone, but which seemed to work for him. He plodded on, never really causing any harm, never becoming dangerous, but simply making a career out of being weird. Then one day, there was the 911 call.

To the middle school mind, a public telephone represents a challenge. If you hit the coin return slot at just the right time, you might find loose, discarded change that would buy your next soda, or a baseball card, or pay your library fine. You might also use the pay phone as a draw for attention. If several other kids are around after a game, a dance, or whatever, and you are the one on the phone, you control the situation. They all hang on your every word, if only so that they can tell how close you are to hanging up so it will be their turn. You can use this time to create a sense of importance for yourself, you can talk back to your parents just for show, or you can coo to a boy on the other end just to make your audience jealous. The possibilities are endless. Perhaps the greatest temptation involving the pay phone, however, is the prank call. This is especially true when it comes to the 911 call. This number, the universal signal for emergencies, seems to drive adults around the world into immediate action, the kind that can liven up any slow day in the hall at school.

We had been having a rash of 911 calls at school and were extremely frustrated by our inability to catch anybody so far. The police were even more frustrated, but of course they showed up every time, only to be told there was no emergency. We gave the usual announcements over the PA, warning of dire consequences for the perpetrator who gets caught, appealing to a sense of community responsibility (e.g., "your house may be being burglarized and the police are up here at school instead of catching the thief"). Nothing worked. Whenever a spell like this hit, it ran its course and then became boring, and the one responsible would go back to vandalizing restrooms or some other form of attention-getting crime.

On this particular day, however, something different happened. The Police Department called me and reported that they had just seconds before received a 911 call and traced it to the pay phone just outside our back door. If I hurried out there, I might see something. Meanwhile, a patrol car was on its way. I immediately went down the hall toward the back door, arriving at the phone not more than 30 seconds after I had hung up my own phone, making it less than a minute since the call had been placed. This was to be my earliest arrival on the scene yet.

When I got there, I was not surprised that the phone looked deserted, but I was surprised to see a student standing nearby, apparently in no hurry to leave the area quickly. It was Stan. I walked calmly up to him and said, "Stan, why are you here?"

"I'm on phone duty," he replied in that weird, overstated voice of his.

"Phone duty?" I asked. "Who put you on 'phone duty'?" (There was no such thing.)

"Mr. Biggers," he answered. (Mr. Biggers was one of my assistants who walked up about this time. He heard what Stan said and shook his head out of the boy's sight.)

Playing along, I said to Stan, "Well, what did he tell you to do?"

"He said to stand here by this phone and make sure nobody uses it."

"So, how long have you been standing here watching?"

"About ten minutes."

"OK, Stan," I said. "Has anybody used the phone during that time?"

"Nope!" was the decisive answer.

"Well, Stan," I said, confident that we had our man. "The police just called and not more than a minute or two ago, they got a 911 call on this phone. Now, if you say you have been here for ten minutes and nobody else has used this phone, but I know that they got that call only two minutes ago, what does that tell me about you?"

Biggers and I studied the odd face of this strange giant, looking for what we were sure would be the signs of an impending confession. After all, my logic was impeccable. There could be no other conclusion. Come on big guy, I thought, tell us what that tells us about you …

Instead, Stan rolled his eyes, thought a second, and answered back. "That I wasn't watching very *closely?*"

Even in the face of overwhelming evidence that he was caught in a crime, Stan could not respond in the expected way. Trying to stifle a laugh, Biggers and I held Stan there until the police arrived. We assigned the usual consequence in this type of case (having to apologize to the officer, get chewed out, and then go to in-school suspension). I am sure that none of that had a long-term logical effect on Stan, but it did stop the calls for a while.

Stan has gone on to high school and will one day graduate, I hope. Tales of his bizarreness sometimes come back to us, as his inability to do the "normal" thing has continued as he has matured. I hope he is socially maturing, albeit at a slower pace, at least sufficiently to get by after he leaves school. He does possess well above-average intelligence. He had a gift for memory and could recite the entire dialogue of a movie in the distinctive voice of each character. I think he has a chance to live a productive life as an adult, if he can just get into an environment where he is not necessarily always expected to do the "normal" thing. He seems headed for a career in either NASA or Hollywood.

Kids like Stan are poised to go either way. We may some-day be buying stock in their companies, using their inventions, or paying to incarcerate them. All we can do in the meantime is to try to teach them to read, to compute, to learn, and to wonder about life. I think we have done all of that we can for Stan. The rest is up to him.

"We need to come in for a conference."

The mother's voice on the phone sounded desperate. She had done all she could, and was now reaching out to the school.

"Karen has changed some of the grades on her report card. We caught her at it and she has confessed. When may we come in?"

As a counselor in a junior high school, in which Karen was one of my seventh-grade students, I was not surprised to hear this kind of thing. I *was* surprised in Karen's case, however, because although I had been seeing her for a couple of months about personal and family problems, I had always known her as a straight-A student.

"How about tomorrow at 3:30?" I answered.

The date was made and I hung up the phone. At first I didn't check, but a few minutes later I said to myself, "Something is not right here," and went to the file. There, on Karen's report card, I saw what I had suspected—straight A's!

At the conference, it all came out. Karen had pretended to lose her report card, but when her parents finally found it in her purse, it had six grades, four A's and two F's, the

F's being in English and Art (I guess she figured two failing grades in two major core curriculum classes would look *too* suspicious). But suspicious they were anyway, because the erasures on the computer-printed slip had been penciled over in a very amateurish way. Karen admitted that she had done this to impress her friends, most of whom had failed at least one course "honestly," but like a rank amateur, she had not thought to change them *after* her parents had seen them.

To Karen's parents, this was an incomprehensible crime. To me, it seemed to fit the pattern of events in the girl's life over the past few weeks. Her visits to my office had become more and more frequent and her tales of experimentation with drugs and hanging out with the fast crowd, unbelievable at first, had become increasingly plausible. This was probably due to the consistency with which she repeated them. Her parents did not understand her, she said. They put enormous pressure on her to excel in school and to be like her older brother, the captain of the football team at the high school where she would go. Her father, a retired air force colonel, pushed her mercilessly, according to her.

Karen did seem to have a lot going for her. She was pretty, well dressed, and popular with the other students. But this school year she had begun to change. She spent less and less time with the honor students, with whom she shared classes, and more time at lunch and after school with the "dopers," the ones everyone at least *thought* were on drugs. Her attitude had begun to suffer and she had been given several opportunities to smoke marijuana, which she had accepted and had come to like, she said. Having noticed in other students who were smoking pot that the first casualty is the attitude, all of this made sense to me. This, coupled with the repeated stories she told me of her abuse of the drug and her parents' emotional abuse of her, made me convinced this girl was looking for help.

Thus, I came to the conference gladly, assuming this was to be the big breakthrough, the day Karen and I would confront her parents with what was going on, a day that we had discussed as inevitable if she wanted real help. Little did I know that I would run into the brick wall that I did.

It is a common practice in school counseling to guard confidentiality as closely as you would in the private sector. The student-client must understand from the beginning, however, that if anything life or health-threatening becomes a major issue that might require outside intervention we must negotiate a way to let the student's family know. Karen knew this, so I don't think she was surprised when I began to steer the conversation toward the activities she and her friends shared, the pressures she felt, and the like. The problem was, she let me do all the talking. She would not admit to anything except changing the grades. After a few minutes of this, I asked if I could see her alone and her parents agreed.

In the next room, Karen and I had a private moment.

"Karen, you know what I'm trying to get at. I think it's time you told them what is going on. Don't worry. I'm here to help. Your parents love you, or they would not be here. It will be okay." I tried to sound at my professional best.

"No, I can't. They won't understand. You don't know them. I don't care what you say. I'll never tell them!" She was crying now, for the first time.

"Then let me try to tell them outright, okay?"

She agreed, reluctantly.

Back in the room with her parents, I began hesitantly to tell them what Karen and I had discussed on her previous visits to my office. I was convinced it was the right thing to do, in view of our confidentiality policy. I was not prepared, however, for what came next.

Karen's stiff, military father and her concerned, naïve mother had been as cooperative as any parent in this type of conference could be up to now. As I began to tell them these things, however, I could see the shift, first in the body language, and then in the tone of the conversation.

"No! This can't be true!" her father said.

"Of course not!" her mother joined in.

I looked at Karen. This time I was the one needing help. She gave me a blank stare.

"Karen, honey, is this true? Have you ever done anything like this?" inquired her incredulous father.

"No, Daddy," she lied. "I never said that. I don't know where he got it."

Back to me.

"So, where did this come from? Why are you telling us this?" he cross-examined me.

"Sir, I promise you. This is exactly what she claims has been happening. I don't know exactly why, but I do know why she doesn't want you to know. She is obviously afraid of displeasing you or disappointing you too much..."

"That's not right. You're making this up for some crazy reason. My daughter knows better than to do drugs. She was not brought up to do that!" he boomed. The mother was now silent. No need to pitch in. The father was on a roll...

"Do you know anything about our family?" he continued. "We have an older son who is an honor student in the high school. He is the quarterback and captain of the football team. I am retired from the air force after twenty years and have my own business. Karen is a brown belt in her karate class. We are very close. We talk about everything we need to. She has everything she needs. Why would a kid like that get involved with drugs? You're way off there, buddy!"

By now, Karen was crying again and being consoled by her shocked mother. I could see that it was a losing effort, but I plodded on, having lost the one ally in the room I thought I had.

"Yes, sir, I know about all of that," I countered. "But I have no reason to make any of this up and don't you think it is unusual that, whether any of this is true or not, Karen is telling this to me as if it were? And of course you know she changed the report card. What about that?"

"That is not an indication that she is on drugs. This little girl has gotten her way too much lately. She has decided she wants to hang out with that longhaired bunch of slugs and wants to impress them. That's all it is. Besides, I think she just wants some attention. Well, I intend to do something about that. Karen, you will not hang out with those kids anymore at all, do you understand?" He was now in charge, back in his comfort zone.

"Yes, Daddy," came the response, through less than sincere tears.

"And as for *you*," he glared at me. "Leave my daughter alone!"

That was it. I never saw Karen in my office again. She avoided me in the halls and moved away within a year, so I never found out what became of her. I learned something, though. I learned that, in situations like that, people have to choose their own time to ask for help. Maybe Karen would have done that (and maybe she did later, anyway) if I had not been so eager to make it happen. I suspect that it came to a head again later, and I hope without further hurt to anyone before help could be found. But I know this: the whole conference occurred because Karen had told a lie once, so I should have known she might do it again. In fact, it later occurred to me that maybe the real truth was, as she said that day, that she never had done anything with drugs. Maybe she had been lying to *me* all along, instead of lying to her parents there in the conference.

I turned off the computer after writing this story, and pondered whether I had made my point about the lesson I had learned. It was time to start a fire in the barbecue grill for a backyard cookout. As I struggled with the lighter fluid, the charcoal and the matches on this windy day, it hit me. I noticed that the wind repeatedly blew out my small match flame every time I dropped it on the pile of black briquettes. Once there was a lull, however, and I could get a little flame going on the surface of the charcoal, the wind actually helped. It took over, fanning the flame and spreading the fire, the way I wanted it to, instead of working against me.

I realized that, in Karen's case, I had been like that wind, coming in too strong when the flame was too small. Subconsciously, I must have known that at the time, because I did not have that happen too many more times. I hope since then I have learned to use the wind wisely, fanning the spirit without snuffing out the spark of what people need to communicate.

One way students try to communicate is by the way they dress. Therefore, one of the toughest parts of being an assistant principal, the head disciplinarian in a school, is enforcing the dress code. Granted, in some public schools you may have visited, you might have thought there was no dress code. But in fact, most schools do have some kind of expected norm for students. It usually involves common sense, decency, safety, and decorum.

Kids and parents often have their own perception of what a dress code should or should not be, and some are bound and determined to practice it at all costs, no matter what the consequences might be.

The clothing and fashion industry also weighs in. They seem always to be pushing the envelope to get kids interested in something edgy, something that might or might not get by mom and dad or the school, but that really looks cool. So, over the years, I have seen short shorts, *really* short shorts (called "Daisy Dukes"), long shorts (sometimes called "Jams"), walking shorts, wind shorts, biker shorts, and probably several other types. Each time we had it pretty well decided what was legal and what was not, the styles would change. As for hair, I have seen long hair, short hair, braided hair, add-ons, extensions, colors, neon colors, shaved heads, half-shaved heads, mohawks, spikes, and some I could not even describe. The same was true there. When the brave ones had tested the rules long enough to be cool, they moved on to something else.

Shirts have evolved too. In the 60s, when I was a teenager, it seemed that most t-shirts were blank. They were sometimes colored, but they were blank with no writing, unless they were a school or team shirt. It was about that time that people began to realize that each of us was wearing through life a whole blank canvas on which countless messages or art could be conveyed to the world. There was an explosion of the so-called message t-shirt.

The t-shirt explosion affected school dress codes significantly. Now it became necessary to monitor what never seemed to need it before. For most schools, tee shirts that were too provocative or controversial with their message became taboo. Thus, a whole new skill had to be developed by administrators. We had to become interpreters of pop-culture slang as well as critics of all kinds of art. Did the use of the word "tool" have a special meaning? It looked pretty innocent on the shirt until you looked closer. Did the placement of a piece of cherry pie in a full-length picture of a leggy waitress have any off-color significance, or was I being a prude if I objected to it?

The problem was, if you figured out what the message was the kids saw you as being too concerned about what to them was no big deal. On the other hand, if you let it slide, they figured they put one over on you and got bolder with their next move.

For example, one day I was looking at a boy's sweatshirt on the playground during lunch. I had seen it before because he wore it every day. It was black with a hood, and had orange and yellow flaming block letters on the front. The letters spelled out, "DECIDE." I had seen it many times and wondered, but thought little of it, even though the kid was a frequent visitor to the office for disciplinary and attitude problems. Still, as the principal and not the assistant at this time, I had not had much direct contact with him.

On this particular day, however, I noticed something different. I called him into my office after lunch and asked him about the shirt.

"It doesn't mean anything," he said, irritated and rolling his eyes at the question. "It's just the name of a band."

"Oh," I said. "What does it say?" (I wanted to hear it in his own words.)

"Decide," he said, looking incredulously at me. "D-E-C-I-D-E!"

I now told him what I had noticed on the playground. "No, it doesn't," I said. "It says, 'DEICIDE'–D-E-I-C-I-D-E." (To most people, the first "I" was not easily seen.)

"That means 'Death to God,'" I told him, "and that is not allowed–too controversial."

So the shirt was not allowed and although his mother fought me on that, the dress code prevailed. It was not that I felt offended or threatened by it. It was just the rule and the next person accused of something similar might be more obvious, but claim they should get by if this kid did.

That's the way it goes with dress codes. They are a necessary evil in schools. It would be nice if parents would cooperate, and they do for the most part, but there are those who seem to have no clue what their kids are wearing to school, or they are being duped by kids who know all the tricks. For example, every girl who wears a too-low-cut blouse knows she should wear a sweater or jacket over it, which she can offer to zip up as soon as someone complains. They all know the trick of carrying other clothes with them in their backpacks or stuffing them in lockers, in case they are told something is not appropriate.

The really ridiculous battles, however, have often centered on hair. From the 60s, when girls who wanted their bangs to be longer than the legal limit actually taped their eyebrows up higher than normal to make the bangs look longer and guys who actually resorted to wearing wigs under which their long hair could hide, to now—kids have been fighting the hair wars. When I first became an assistant principal, the district in which I worked had rules about boys' hair that had to do with how close to the collar it could come, how far down on the face, and so on. Over the years, they had to evolve to say things like "no distractive hair styles or hair coloring." That helped, but still left much interpretation up to the administrator.

My own view was that the hair wars had been fought and won or lost (depending on where you stood) in the 70s, and what I wanted was to see their hair be "clean and not green." I always insisted that if you were going to color your hair, it had to be some kind of natural color. When asked what a natural color was, I would say, "Anything that someone, somewhere, was born with." You would think that would exclude the blues and greens and pinks, but we always had arguments over maroons, magentas, etc. I had a girl once who came to school with such a bad dye job that I felt sorry for her. She had magenta hair, a magenta neck, ears, and fingers. Her silly appearance was its own punishment.

This is where dress codes get tough to enforce. A girl showed up one day with the left half of her head shaved. The other side was still shoulder length. One of her teachers was livid, demanding to know what I was going to do. I said, "I don't know–make her shave the other side?" We eventually did just that, and allowed her to wear a hat (another dress code violation) for a while as it grew back.

Over the years, I found that the main reason kids defied the dress code was a manifestation of something we were trying to teach them anyway–personal responsibility and expression–they were just choosing inappropriate ways and times to do it. It became clear that in many cases, if we just acknowledged that they had gotten our attention and now needed to get back to business, they would comply.

One such case was that of Chris. He was an eighth-grader known more as a class clown than anything else. He got into minor trouble regularly, but was by far not the worst case in school. As principal, I had dealt with him on enough occa-sions to know him. One morning, as I was leaving the cam-pus for a meeting, one of my assistant principals called me into her office. She had Chris there and she asked me what I thought of his hairstyle for the day. Chris, whose straight, brown hair was only two or three inches long, had put it all up in tiny pigtails, each secured with brightly colored rubber bands, all over his head. He actually looked pretty silly, kind of like the clown he liked to be.

I said, "No, Chris. You can't do that and go to class. Get rid of those," and left with Rose, my assistant, assuring me she would take care of it.

At the end of the day, as I came back into the building, here came Rose with Chris. If it had been appropriate, I am sure she would have been leading him by his ear, she was so mad at him.

"I want you to see this," she said to me. "I made him fix this this morning and now look!" she exclaimed.

Chris's hair had exactly the same appearance it had when I had left that morning. I was livid. "That does it!" I said. "You are suspended for tomorrow, then you can come back as long as you do not wear it that way again." I called his mother, who could be difficult, and explained that I would not have suspended him for the hair, I was suspending him for the defiance and insubordination. She, a teacher herself, had to agree.

I thought that was it until the next morning, when a teacher came up to me before school, jerked her head toward the playground where the eighth-graders congregated each morning and said, "You might want to see this before they go to class."

I walked outside and was not sure whether to laugh or cry. Eight of Chris's friends, all girls, had put their hair up into the same kind of pigtails as his! They were attracting attention already, but were sure to be an even bigger distraction when they went to class. I walked into the middle of them and asked what this was all about. They said it was

not fair that their friend got suspended and they were showing their support for him. I asked them if they thought his
suspension was for the hairstyle and they all said yes. I then
explained that I would not have suspended him for that, but
I did suspend him for the defiance he showed by correct-
ing it and then redoing it behind my back. Although this
made sense to them I am sure, they all stuck to their protest
except for one, who was the daughter of the Parent Teacher
Organization (PTO) president and decided not to endure
the phone call she knew I was about to make.

The rest accompanied me to the office. I showed them
the nine-foot church pew I had bought when we moved in
for kids to sit on while waiting in there (a subtle reminder of
suggested penitence) and told them to have a seat. "All right,
if you want to have your little protest, you can, but not in the
hall or in class. It is going to be right here. Have a seat on the
pew. There is a big window here, so people can see you when
they walk by. But if you prefer, you can take that stuff out of
your hair right now and go to class. Meanwhile, I am going
to call your parents…"

The girls all sat down, but Chris's best friend Allen, who
had been around but not involved (i.e., nothing in his hair),
started prancing around the office, spouting all kinds of
rhetoric about freedom of expression, the Bill of Rights, and
the like. He would not shut up. Meanwhile, the bell rang to
go to class. I said, "Allen, are you part of this group? If you
are not, go to class. If you are, here are some rubber bands.
Put some in your hair and have a seat with your friends!"

Allen looked puzzled, then quickly said, "Nah, I gotta go
to class, man," and left. So much for commitment to a cause.

When I had finished the eight phone calls, each parent had agreed with me that this was a bit much and asked me to tell their kids they expected them to drop the protest and go to class. I told them I would talk it over with all the girls, which I did. We talked and they began to understand and one by one the rubber bands came out. They all went back to class and were never heard from again.

What these girls learned from that experience was a secondary issue to the dress code thing and a more important one. They learned that there is a proper way to express yourself and an improper way. They learned, I hope, that rules like dress codes are there because people need them, and at some point you have to pick what battles you want to fight (that goes for both sides).

What I really have never understood, however, is the way adults, in some cases, dress when it comes to school. As an assistant principal years ago, I was told by my principal that I needed to talk to a teacher about the tight, white pants she was wearing in class, partly because they were too revealing of her rather large figure, but also because she tended to wear dark-colored panties underneath, which just magnified the problem. It was so bad that even the adolescent boys in her classes were offended! When the people on campus who house in their bodies more pent-up hormones than anyone within miles are turned off by this display, you know it is gross. And it was.

I don't remember what I said to that woman, but I guess it worked. She changed her wardrobe, if not her style, and we got through the year. A similar incident later lasted several years, with a good teacher who just could not understand why the boys were always either looking at her too much or complaining about the way she dressed.

Parents are worse. I have seen people show up at school in pajamas, house coats, robes, slippers, and plain old bare feet. One grossly overweight woman known to be especially rough came in wearing biker shorts that strained to contain her bulk, no shoes, tattoos everywhere, and a loose tank top with no bra that showed cleavage that should have handrails to keep people from falling in. Add to this some dirty, scraggly hair, and you get the picture. She was there to let me know her son could do no wrong.

Another time, my assistant Terry called me into his office to help deal with an irate mother and her husband. The woman was standing and doing all the talking while the man sat passively in a chair. A pile of jeans shorts had been plopped down angrily on Terry's desk, and the mother was enraged. Terry had called her to tell her that her daughter's shorts were too short according to our dress code and she would need to bring her something else to wear.

"What do you mean? How dare you tell me her shorts are too short!" she bellowed. They are just fine. *This* would be too short!" She hiked her own dress up to a point that made Terry blush.

She went on, "My daughter has five pairs of these shorts," she said, pointing to the pile, "and I paid fifty dollars for each one of them, and you are going to tell me she can't wear them to school?"

Terry looked up at her from his chair, then at me. Neither of us was sure of the next move. Finally, I looked at the dad, who had said nothing, but I had suddenly noticed he was getting more interested. "What do you think, sir?" I asked.

Building up some steam of his own, the man leaned forward in his chair, fixed his gaze on his wife, and boomed, "I want to know why my daughter has *five* pairs of *fifty-dollar shorts!*"

That started an argument between the two of them that Terry and I backed away from. As they left, still barking at each other, the woman mumbled something about taking her daughter home to change.

My favorite, however, was the day when two secretaries came to my door, trying to suppress giggles, and told me that a parent wanted to see me at the front desk, which I could not see from my office as the assistant principal. I walked out to see the woman, who turned out to be an older sister of a student, not the parent. I am not sure that made a difference, because what I found myself staring at was just as startling either way. There at the counter stood an attractive, well-built young woman in a *string bikini*.

"May I help you?" I managed to say, after I caught my breath.

"Yes, I wanted to pick up my little brother for an appointment," (something she could have done easily without me, but now I could see why the secretaries had insisted that I see her. I thought I could hear giggling somewhere behind me).

"OK, just sign the book and…" I started, "and we–"

She cut me off. "I don't think I should go down the hall like this, do you?" she made a failed attempt to cover herself with her arms.

"No," I said, trying to look no lower than her neck. I looked elsewhere and said, "It might be best if you wait in the car." She agreed and left. Feeling my face turning redder by the minute, I tried to make it to my office before the laughter of six women erupted. The two secretaries were especially pleased with themselves.

Parents and their kids are not much different sometimes when it comes to rules. Whatever happens—sagging pants, tight pants, shaved hair, long hair—there will always be a need for some kind of standard for dress in schools. And wherever there is a dress code, there will always be someone there to challenge it.

A Visit from the Kings of the Hill

"We'll be there Thursday," the voice on the phone said. I hung up in disbelief. The call had come from a person unknown to me. He was a comic writer in town for a convention. He and his friends had picked our school (a new middle school of which I was principal) as a place to visit to get ideas. They were the writing team for a popular animated television show called *King of the Hill.*

If you have never seen it, I should explain that *King of the Hill* is a look at life in a middle-class, small-town or suburban setting. The town of Arlen is said to be modeled after Austin (we were in Pflugerville, a northern suburb of Austin). Other towns have also claimed to be the inspiration, I have heard, but I am not sure the creators are saying. The show focuses on Hank Hill, his wife Peggy, and their son, Bobby, who at the beginning of the series, anyway, was in middle school. The writers chose to come to us because they were looking for new ideas for stories.

I was both flattered and fascinated with the idea of the visit, but not sure what they were looking for. When the six men showed up, all of them under 30 and very casually dressed, I took them around the campus and explained whatever we saw. I watched their reactions to the building, the kids, and the things I told them. They were pretty calm, just nodding and occasionally laughing. I was trying hard to resist the tendency most people have to make a fool of themselves when talking to a celebrity.

And I did consider them celebrities. I did not know any of them, but had seen their work and at times thought it was brilliant. It was at least always entertaining. I thought how enjoyable it would be to have a job where all you have to do is be funny.

So, as we went around the campus, I tried to come up with other ideas, but the one I had already had before they came seemed to be the best. In the show, Hank is a "good ol' boy," a "redneck," who sells propane gas for a living, wears clean white t-shirts and jeans, and drinks a lot of beer in the backyard with his buddies, all of whom are stereotypical characters themselves. It had occurred to me that, with the revolution in our curriculum that was going on at the time, there might be a story for these writers. It would have to do with the changes in the way we teach something that used to be called "shop."

Over the years, "shop" (education in the use of power tools to create woodworking projects) had evolved. It had been renamed "Industrial Arts" in the 1970s, and eventually, now that we were in the 90s when the comic writers visited, became known as Technology Education. The subjects covered had increased greatly from simple woodworking to robotics, computer-aided drafting, power, and several others. And the teachers had evolved too. Whereas the shop teacher I had in middle school in the 60s was a crusty old guy who was missing two fingers, we now had sharply-dressed, young idealists coming out of school intent on helping kids understand the world of working technology and industry.

So, with this mind, I told the writers, "What if you had Bobby coming home telling his dad he was in one of these classes and explaining that his first project would be to create a model city using something like popular plastic building blocks to show how a city should be laid out or to build a rocket ship out of cardboard? All this while Hank is thinking Bobby is going to come home with a birdhouse or a gun rack, or at least a cutting board for his mom, like I made way back when. This might give rise to an interesting conflict between Hank and the school."

The writers nodded and seemed to agree somewhat, but nobody shoved a contract under my nose and asked me to pack for Hollywood. They looked at the lab where we taught Tech. Ed. and made some notes. Little did I know that in a few months, friends of mine would see that episode, or something resembling it, played out on the screen. I have yet to see it myself.

But the real surprise of the day, during their visit, came in the hallway. We had a student at the time that had numerous problems. He had a learning disability, he was slow-talking, slow-walking, and had a funny way his voice cracked when he talked because, being in the seventh grade, he was right between a child's voice and what would become his lower, man's voice. He was chubby, round-faced with short brown hair and a sense of wonder at all he saw. In other words, he was just like Bobby. In fact, we secretly called him "Bobby," because the resemblance was so striking.

Now, walking down an empty hall with these six writers, I saw something they just had to see. It was our "Bobby" coming down the hall by himself. I turned to the writers while "Bobby" was still out of earshot and said, "You should watch this."

This kid and I knew each other, so it was not unusual that I would stop to talk to him. "Where you going?" I asked.

"Restroom." He held up a doorknob his teacher used as a token pass (an object bearing the teacher's name and given to students when they are called to the office or sent on an errand).

"OK," I said. "But don't stay out of class too long. Are you doing okay in your classes?"

"Yes, sir," he answered politely. In his slow drawl, he filled in a few more details, while I watched the faces of the writers.

Stunned. To a man, they were stunned. The longer "Bobby" talked, the farther their jaws dropped. When he finally shuffled off to the restroom, one of them spoke.

"I don't believe it," he said. "Bobby is real! We thought we made him up!"

They say life imitates art, or is it the other way around? In this case, without even knowing it, these creative guys had crafted a fictitious model of something that already existed in real life. To me, this was one more example of how school is where *real* life takes place.

The writers went back and wrote their stories. Someday I hope to see the one I gave them the idea for. As for my efforts, all I got was a free tee shirt from the show, but I will be ready for these guys when they run out of ideas again.

Jack was big. He was only in the eighth grade, but he was bigger than many full-grown men. Standing about five-foot-ten and weighing over two hundred pounds, he was proud of his size. Jack was not a great athlete, so he did not capitalize on his girth on the field or the court, but used it to compensate for something which made him feel less than adequate —his right hand.

Jack's right hand was somehow deformed at birth, I guess. I never did hear the full story, but everyone knew that the hand was not right. It looked all right from one angle, then he would turn it and you would see how the fingers went off in strange directions and only the pincer grip, between the thumb and forefinger, worked normally. To most middle-schoolers, it was downright scary, and a smaller person with such a deformity would have been the subject of much ridicule. In big Jack's case, they quietly called it "the claw."

Now Jack was otherwise troubled too. He just would not admit it. Living with a weak mother and a distant, emotionally abusive stepfather, Jack came to school angry most of the time. He disrupted classes, he shirked responsibilities, he failed academically, and when he got bored, he got into fights.

It was always easy for Jack to get into fights. As his assistant principal in his middle school of over twelve hundred students, I saw Jack often and I saw the explosive temper erupt over any slight suggestion that he had done something wrong. Ironically, of all the things his teachers and I accused him of or his peers clashed with him about, none of them ever had anything to do with his hand, the one area where he could *not* be blamed and might have had a *right* to feel persecuted. Instead, he never accepted responsibility for his actions, choosing to defend himself blindly and sometimes stupidly, even in the face of overwhelming evidence of his own culpability.

One day, having been charged with a serious theft of a favorite paperweight right off the desk of the counselor who was trying to help him, he came completely unglued. In his claw grip he held a piece of wood that his teacher used for a token pass. As I confronted Jack with the evidence and made him cough up the missing paperweight, he became so angry at me that he threw the block of wood at the desk between us. It hit the desktop and bounced over my left shoulder and against the wall. No harm done, but I got a new appreciation for the power of this rather large, out-of-control adolescent. Another time, he picked up that same desk in a fit of rage and slammed it down. It was usually like that when Jack got mad.

That's when Chase came. This new student was a stark contrast to Jack. In fact, if two kids could be more opposite, they would have had to be written into the comics. Chase was from California. He was cool. He was of average build, had one of those short-toward-the-back and long-in-the-front hairstyles. His straight, light brown locks hung to one side and just below his left eye so that you could never tell what it was doing. He constantly played with those bangs, pushing them back over his ear, then seeming to be amused at the adults who stared, waiting for all that hair to rush forward and cover his eye again at the slightest movement of his head. But it was *style.*

Chase had the girls right where he wanted them too. While Jack had his troubles even getting girls to look at him, Chase needed a secretary to keep up with his calls. His California cool and his constant talk about surf and sun and skateboards and sailboats frustrated Jack's Texas drawl and small-town bully image. They were so different, they were bound to clash.

I don't remember what started it. Chase certainly had had, after a short while, his share of crises in my office. His approach, however, was different. Instead of throwing things or picking up desks, he usually cursed me and the system and ran. We always found him (once with the help of the police) and brought him back to justice. On this particular day, though, he and Jack ended up in my office together because they had finally met in combat. Maybe Chase had popped off once too often about California. Maybe Jack had teased him about his hair. Whatever it was, they now sat across from me and waited for their fate.

After handing out suspensions for both of these guys, I began the usual process of trying to counsel them toward better options than fighting. While their eyes rolled and they slumped in their chairs, I told them about how all adults, even teachers, don't always get along, but you don't usually see them squared off in the hall. About how the older you get, it becomes more important what you know and how you use it, not whom you can whip. Anyway, I explained that they did not have to be friends, but needed very much (for their sake as well as mine) to get along. I asked if they could agree to disagree, to give each other their own space, to live and let live, to—well, you get the idea. By this time, they would have agreed to anything that would have freed them from my lecture.

Having gotten a commitment from both boys toward better behavior and peaceful coexistence, at least for the near future, I asked them, "Okay, you guys, when grown men agree on something, what do they do?" Jack seemed puzzled. Chase hesitated only slightly, then extended his hand toward Jack—his *left* hand. It was a small gesture, one that might have been lost in the emotional steam quickly evaporating from the room, but Jack noticed. He immediately softened. He took that left hand in his, avoiding the awkward scene of trying to seal this new agreement with the claw, and he and Chase both smiled. Nobody said a word to draw attention to the gesture directly, but all three of us grasped its significance. Chase, for all of his irritating arrogance, had shown in one brief moment that he already had the kind of respect for Jack that I had not been able to preach into him over the last fifteen minutes, nor in the last fifteen visits to my office. When I called her, Chase's worn-out single mother could do little more than cry and thank me for noticing that her son was capable of doing the right thing. The two never fought again.

About four years later, I ran into Chase in a grocery store. He was a stock boy, working his way through the community college. He spoke to me calmly, maturely, made the kind of

awkward small talk adults make, and then he asked me a
surprising question. He said, "Of all of the kids you have
dealt with, did anybody ever act worse than me?" I brushed
the question off with some kind of lame joke. We parted, and
as I walked down the aisle of the store and remembered that
small gesture in my office years earlier, I thought, "Worse
than you, Chase? You bet. Much, *much* worse."

It was the first week of school, 1980. Two seventh-grade boys met each other for the first time and stood talking in the school cafeteria. They were having one of those adolescent conversations in which material possessions of each are compared, a few names are dropped, and sometimes, to gain an edge, the relative worth of the male parent is brought up. This kind of rooster strutting is never effective unless it is witnessed by a fair number of male peers, who serve as a kind of jury which decides who one-upped whom. Surrounded by just such a group, the pair engaged in this time-honored ritual in the following manner:

"Well, my dad has a job at a computer place and he's got a deer lease and lots of guns and we go huntin' almost every weekend when he comes to see me."

"Yeah? Well, my dad goes out of town on weekends a lot, but when he comes back he brings me a big stack of baseball cards and sometimes a whole bunch of comic books. He's got guns, too, and sometimes he lets me shoot 'em, but the thing I like best is his car. He's got a *bad* car! It'll go from zero to sixty in about five seconds. Man, it's *awesome!*"

"My dad's car is fast, too. He even lets me drive it some-times, but he says he has to be careful 'cause he let somebody drive it once and they really messed it up. You have to take care of a Trans Am. They cost a lot–"

"Your dad has a Trans Am? What color is it?"

"Black, with chrome wheels, and–"

"No joke? What year, man?" The voice was cracking with an impending sense of doom.

"'79. Why?"

"Man, I don't believe this! My dad's car is exactly like that! And what's weird is I wrecked it one time. Oh, man! This is too much! Where does your dad live … ?"

You know the rest. Somehow this father had managed to keep the existence of his son and his stepson a complete secret to both of them for quite some time. The scene turned awkwardly pathetic. The "jury" shuffled their feet, snickered a little, and rather quickly disbanded. One of the boys dissolved into tears, while the other used a nervous laughter to hide his embarrassment. Soon, both were in the counselor's office.

Since both boys were clients of the other counselor in the school, I never heard the rest of the story in detail. I know that it took them a long while to get over that initial shocking meeting and to accept their individual situations. One of them eventually moved to another school. I always remembered their pain, though, and I even felt a little sorry for their two-timing father/stepfather. Far be it from me to pass judgment on the guy's motives, but his methods obviously left something to be desired. I just remember how sad it was that, until their two worlds came to this unfortunate collision, these two boys seemed pretty normal.

I wondered if they ever had an idea of how much they were being deceived. Did they know more than they let on, and just tried to act "normal" to save face? Were they, in effect, practicing a kind of deception of their own? What good can come out of a system that encourages parents to deceive their kids and kids to deceive themselves?

A friend of mine in the mental health field recently told me that he had heard of a wise divorce court judge who said to a couple of parents:

"I will grant this divorce and will accept the suggested parental visitation arrangements, with one exception. *You, the parents, will move.* Your children and their belongings will stay where they are. Their friends will remain the same. Their school will not change. Their routine will not be disrupted. Their daily value system will not be shattered. This was *your* idea, so if you want it bad enough, you will both move out and take turns moving back in periodically to lend some sense of parenthood to the household."

Brave man, that judge (and a few since then). I hope he made it stick. Why isn't this done more often? If everybody who wanted to get divorced had to do it this way, would we have as many of them as we do? Isn't this more fair to the ones who are often victimized the most? The judge deserves a medal.

That meeting in the cafeteria was 28 years ago. Those two boys are grown, probably with families of their own by now. Did their experience make them want to hold those families together, or did it teach them how to take them apart without telling everyone involved about it?

Deception. Some divorces are caused by it. Some are perpetuated by it. Either way, that judge may have been on to something. If a divorce seems to be necessary, then let's see what a little honesty up front about it can do for the ones often likely to suffer the most—the children.

Walton Falls for the Bluff

There is something about an expensive pair of basketball shoes that attracts an adolescent like puppies attract women. They just cannot keep their hands off them and most of the time, they just have to *have* them. That must have been the case with Walton and these shoes, because of the pain he went through to try to get them and then to keep them.

Walton was a seventh grader with a pile of problems. In his large middle school, he was failing miserably; in trouble all of the time, he never seemed to know just how serious his situation was. Still, he imagined himself a student athlete. He was not really going to be able to keep his grades up enough to stay eligible, but he came out for the team at the beginning of each season, anyway. Sure enough, by the end of the first six-week grading period, he was not allowed to play, or even to practice with the team anymore.

So it was that Walton found himself with a great deal of time on his hands. Since supervision and guidance for him had never been the strong suit of his single, working mother, he was left pretty much to his own devices to stay entertained and occupied after school. That may be one reason Walton decided to take up with Jaydon.

Jaydon (pronounced "Jay–DAHN") was quite a character. He was older than Walton (tenth grade, for the second year) and went to a high school in a neighboring district. Jaydon had a police record longer than his 1979 Camaro, which he drove to our campus every day after school was out to pick up Walton, now that the poor young man was a "child in need of supervision," as the courts would call him.

It was never clear to me whether they were related or just friends, but Jaydon and Walton had a bond of some kind that I suspected was somehow a little bit criminal. Jaydon was not really the kind of kid most mothers would have sought out as a companion for their bored son, but I can see how she might have fallen for his line.

You see, I had known Jaydon when I was a counselor at his high school a couple of years before. During that time, I had tried to help him, but he did not need help. He knew everything. He knew so much that it did not matter to him that the girl he was flirting with when he was a freshman was the girlfriend of a senior who did not take it lightly. It did not matter to him that he had insulted the guy in some conversation about this flirting incident and had become the only kid I had ever seen get literally chased off the campus by a senior and his friends, who were throwing *lit firecrackers* at him. Nope, he knew *everything*.

And you could believe him. Jaydon could smile (he was a good-looking kid) and tell you the world was flat and you would, at least for a moment, be tempted to doubt Magellan. He had a sense of humor, a quick wit, and a charm that was irresistible when he was giving his side of some ridiculously bogus story.

Now I was the assistant principal in this middle school and dealing with Walton on a daily basis. You can imagine how surprised I was to find out that Jaydon was the new self-appointed protector of "his man" Walton.

So, what about the shoes? It seems that one day, before I knew Jaydon was at all involved with our school in any way, he arrived to pick up Walton and did not find him waiting at the curb this time. Walton was nowhere to be seen, so Jaydon got out to look for him. They hooked up somewhere near the locker room and decided to go in and "look around." They found an open door and went in, and there they were—a brand new pair of Michael Jordan red, white, and black high tops. At the time, they were the most expensive basketball shoes on the market. They were absolute beauty and perfection. They were style, they were grace, they were money, and in a flash, they were Walton's.

Within minutes, Walton and Jaydon were out the door and on the street with their prize. Looking back, I really think Walton, younger and simpler than Jaydon, would have kept the shoes for himself. After all, he had seen them, he had taken them, and Jaydon was only the getaway driver. The sad thing is, Walton would probably have been just simple enough to wear them to school the next day. But Jaydon the Protector would have none of that. They made other plans for the shoes, and then began the Great Investigation.

There are a few things it is wise to handle gently: a sleeping pit-bull, a dirty diaper, and a parent whose kid's shoes have been stolen at school. This guy, the father of the shoes' owner, was livid. He cursed the principal. He threatened lawsuits. He came storming up to the school demanding his rights. He ranted and raved about his one-hundred-dollar-plus investment being lost, about the unlocked door, etc. The principal gave me, the person in charge of discipline at the school, the job of finding out who took the shoes.

In a school of eight hundred and fifty students, it would be impossible to accomplish this task if it were not for one valuable tool–The Snitch. After a week of calling people in and asking if anybody had seen anything, I finally found a couple of these valuable little guys. They had both been in the locker room, were not together, and both gave identical stories about seeing Walton and "some high school guy" in the locker room looking at the shoes and then stuffing them into a backpack.

There were a few other things Walton could not account for (he had been questioned earlier in the week as a prime suspect), such as exactly where he was after school that day, but nothing had stuck. Now, with these two independent but identical stories, I knew we had something. Not much, but something. Besides, these little guys could probably be believed, because the shoes were admittedly left out in the open on a bench instead of locked in a locker (something the ranting father never confronted his son with) and yet these two had never considered taking them themselves.

So, with this little bit of information, I went back to Walton. In the meantime, I had found out that Walton had a probation officer. For some reason, the revelation of that did not bowl me over. I decided it was time to try The Bluff.

Now, The Bluff works like this: you call the person in and you start with the assumption that you know something he doesn't. You work it in that since you know this information, you will have to turn it over to someone of authority who can do something about it. That is supposed to get the desired result–in this case a confession and a return of the goods. At this point, I was more interested in the latter so I could see justice done and get that parent off our backs. This did not work in Walton's case, however, because he seemed completely unfazed. No confession. No shoes. In fact, he seemed a little surprised himself that he even *had* a probation officer. Ironically, the whole thing might have ground to a halt right there if it were not for one factor–Jaydon.

This was the point at which I learned about the Jaydon Connection. Jaydon's name had first come up when Walton and I had our first conversation about the shoes. As he had tried to explain where he was on that day, he had mentioned that Jaydon was picking him up after school. My raised eyebrows had told Walton (perceptive one that he was) that I knew Jaydon (how many Jaydons are there?) and that this could be useful information, although not for the purpose of exonerating poor Walton.

"Jaydon?" I asked. "I know him. I used to be his counselor. I haven't seen him in a couple of years. Why was he picking you up?"

"He picks me up every day. He takes me home. My mama knows about it," explained Walton.

Now, in our follow-up conversation a week into the Investigation, we were discussing all of this right after school one day. I had called Walton in right at the end of the day and was making him late to meet Jaydon.

Having answered my questions satisfactorily (he thought) and determining that he did not know he had a probation officer to whom I could tell anything, Walton squirmed in his chair.

"Can I go?" he asked. "Jaydon's probably out there right now."

It was now about 4:00. I said okay, but then added, "Why don't you tell Jaydon to come in tomorrow when he picks you up and we will talk about this. In the meantime, see if you can find those shoes and bring them to me."

"I ain't got the shoes, man, and you better quit sayin' I do. I'm gonna get Jaydon to …" His voice trailed off as he left.

Next day, right after the last bell, here comes Jaydon with his little charge at his side.

"Hey, why you been hasslin' my man Walton, here?"

(Hello, Jaydon, nice to see you again, too.)

"I'm not hassling him," I said. "I just told him that I knew he had taken those shoes and I want them back. I said if he didn't give them back, I would let his probation officer handle it."

Now, this is something curious about The Bluff. It works better on *smart* people. Jaydon and Walton had not exactly bonded because of a mutual interest in joining Mensa, but Jaydon could at least spell it, whereas poor Walton …

So Jaydon listened to The Bluff and it kind of made sense. He knew something Walton probably did not grasp— that true Snitches rarely lie. He also knew the system and I could see him mentally counting his losses. Still, he tried another angle.

"Naw, man, you don't understand," he said. "Those shoes are on the street by now. Walton couldn't get 'em back if he wanted to. They're gone."

"Tell it to the probation officer," I said. "Or better yet, if those shoes are not on my desk by the end of the day tomorrow, I'll tell him myself." (Now I was really bluffing. I didn't even know the guy's name yet.)

They left my office with a lot of mumbling, "Yeah, right man, sure … "

I closed up my office and headed for a meeting with some teachers down the hall, to which I was late because of what I was now sure was my failed attempt at The Bluff. About an hour later, I was called to the door of the room in which we were meeting. I was surprised to see a very agitated Jaydon at the door. He was breathing a little heavy and doing a sort of "posturing" dance in the hall.

"There go your shoes, man," he exclaimed, pointing toward the floor. "Now, leave my man Walton alone, okay?"

I looked down in amazement to see the beauty and perfection of the red, white, and black Jordans. "Thanks, Jaydon," I managed to say.

"Well, it ain't right, man. I hope you're happy." Pointing to his own wrist, he said, "I had to give up my Guess watch to get those things back. It just ain't right," he growled, while he pranced around the hall.

"I'm sorry, Jaydon," I said. "Why don't you call the police?"

He almost laughed, but with a spin on his heel and flip of his middle finger, he was gone in a hail of profanity and I never saw him again.

Walton was suspended from school for five days and Mr. Investment got his shoes back (for which he never thanked the principal or me). I wish I could say that Jaydon and Walton saw the error of their ways and left the street gang life they had chosen for something more positive, but somehow I doubt it. I don't even know if Walton ever met with his probation officer again. Frankly, I never knew for sure if there *was* one.

Let's Talk about Football, 1965-66

My own journey included my learning experience with the game of football, which began in the seventh grade. I was very excited about playing on the school team, but not very confident of my abilities. I remember getting called over by the coach a few minutes before my first game. He told me I was to start at left end. I was thrilled and terrified at the same time. So terrified, in fact, that I forgot to go out on the field after we received the opening kickoff! The only other highlight of that game that I remember is my clipping penalty that nullified a touchdown run. After that game, I did not start.

Time went by and I spent most of it on the sidelines. Luckily, we had a good team, so I nearly always got to play at least a little through the rest of junior high school. By the time I reached high school, though, my skills and my confidence had improved enough that I became a regular starter when I was a junior.

Now the situation had reversed itself. I was a starter, but I was on a really *bad* team. Even at that, I much preferred being a starter to "riding the pine," as they say. Thankfully in football, as opposed to basketball, you don't really *sit* on the bench, you mostly *stand* on the sideline, and you have a helmet you can put on so nobody sees your face. In basketball, you have to sit there with everybody witnessing your hopeful plea as the coach looks down the line for a sub. When you do finally get in, you are known as someone less than cool (at least for skinny white boys like me) by the red marks on your knees, where your elbows have rested during your long periods of inactivity. It's embarrassing, but you deal with it because you love the game.

So here I was playing all the time and doing pretty well, but the team was *terrible*. Still, I kept pinching myself. *Me, a starter*, I said to myself. My older brother had preceded me by three years and several touchdowns and he had had it both ways–a starter and on a very good team. In fact, he was not just a starter; he was bona fide *star* material. He went on to play college and semi-professional football and to be a very successful coach. But for me, just to start, even on the doormat of the state, was an accomplishment.

And we were just about that–the doormat of the state of Texas. My junior year we had a perfect record–no wins, ten losses. Every week we got the same speech about "breaking into the win column" from our well-meaning coach, who had inherited this defending district championship team, but who we were sure already had his U-haul trailer packed by mid-October.

It was not that we could not play the game. We just couldn't score. I was rather proud of the fact that by the seventh game of the season I was tied for high-point man on the team, but I played *defense*. Even at that, I had only one touchdown. We were *worse* than bad.

The last game of the year, which could not come soon

enough, was to be played against Ryder High School in Wichita Falls. This was the team our guys had beaten the year before for the championship. They had an American Indian tailback named Bub Deerinwater, who had been a junior in that big game. Deerinwater was a name that struck fear into the heart of every defensive back in the district. Although we jokingly called him a "legend in his own mind," he had a whole library of folklore that preceded him into every stadium. "This guy grew up in a teepee and hunted bear with a bow and arrow," or "I hear he runs home from school every day, five miles through the woods, barefooted, uphill both ways," they would say. "I heard his grandfather was the great Jim Thorpe," the stories went on and the mystique grew larger than life. We envisioned him as the perfect American Indian hero. Trying to defeat him would be like rooting against Abe Lincoln. We were, as they say, "psyched out."

This being the case, and given the fact that the closest we could come on our team to such romanticism was a guy on our second string who once *visited* an Indian reservation, we were in trouble. As we cowered our way into the last week of the season, there were some heroic efforts aimed at inspiring us to turn this situation to our advantage. "They're over-confident," our coaches would say. "They're in for a big surprise." "They'll be sorry." One coach even delivered an impassioned plea at the pep rally for everyone to come to Wichita Falls (90 miles away) and witness "the biggest upset in the history of Texas high school football." Fortunately, most of them stayed home.

You would have thought that a guy like Deerinwater would have been itching to avenge the dramatic loss of the previous year. Wrong! They didn't even *play* him! They did not want to take a chance on injuring their star right before the playoff season. They had the championship sewn up this time before they even got to us. Now we were to be the dessert for all those subs on their team who had stood on the sidelines like I used to do, napkin at the neck, knife and fork in hand, waiting for the final dish. The Legend spent the entire game on the sidelines. It's funny—I spent all those games in junior high standing on the sidelines, waiting for my big chance, and now he was doing it for one game and getting kudos for it.

Despite our overdose of inspiration, the night went pretty much as expected. Deerinwater never even got his kneepads dirty and probably did not need a shower after the game. As a defensive back, my anticipated head-on clash with the Legend, of course, never materialized. Instead, I received the dubious honor of being run over by the "Guy Who *Subbed For* the Legend." It was a good old-fashioned Texas waxing. The score was 35–0, but it was not nearly that close. The best thing about the night for us was that the season was finally *over*.

With that disaster finished, we came back the next year (yes, we actually came back) with a new attitude. All of us were smarting but determined to gain some respect. By the end of the season our record, 1–7–2, did not look much better, but there were some bright spots. We had actually won a game, we had tied the fifth-ranked team in the state, and we had compiled enough scoring statistics that at least no one could memorize them.

Why didn't we win more? We calculated that if we had scored one more touchdown in each game, our record would have been 8–2. Furthermore, we were ahead going into the last quarter in all but two games. It seemed that, given the experience of the year before, we were convinced we were losers. As the game wound down, if we were ahead, we began to expect disaster and usually got it. I remember that feeling coming over me a few times on the field and not really knowing what to do to shake it.

What did I learn from these experiences with this sport I loved but which frustrated me so? The team for which I would endure all kinds of humiliation from critics just for the right to suit up with? Expectations. It became clear that merely expecting to win would not work (we had tried that), but every week we saw that expecting to lose almost always produced the intended result.

I looked back later and saw, as each reunion passed and we team members would remember how bad we were, that the important thing was not that we kept getting knocked down, but that we always got back up. We were by no means the first to learn this. We carried on the time-honored tradition of finishing the race. That is even biblical (2 Timothy 4:7). We finished a hard season; we put it behind us and hoped we would never see it again. But the things we learned there made us who we became.

I sat there on the locker room floor after my final game of my senior year and cried all over my shoulder pads. I did not yet know whether I would ever wear them again, but whatever happened, I was determined never to think of myself as a loser again.

My next big tryout would be for the job of teacher, where I would find that expectations played an even bigger role in the determination of the outcome. I could not bring about success in the classroom just by expecting it, but I could surely keep a kid down by not ever expecting him to rise above the Legends poised to run over him.

My football career was a bittersweet time filled with team disasters and individual triumphs. It may not have produced trophy-lined dens where legends are perpetually celebrated, but the life lessons I learned could have their own section in the library. I would not even trade them for a winning season.

It has been said that experience is what you get when you do not get what you wanted. In my own journey through school, when it came to football especially, I had gotten plenty of that. It turned out to be one of the best teachers I ever had.

A Lesson in Life from the Laundromat

It was cold outside. Cold, and for the umpteenth time in the last two months, I was on my way to the Laundromat at eleven o'clock at night. We had just moved into a brand new house and were having the weirdest problem—our dryer vent was flooding every time the sky even looked cloudy. For some reason, the builder had put the clothes dryer vent pipe under the concrete slab foundation. This meant that it came out exactly at ground level, and well, you can figure it out from there. It seemed that this lovely little problem always presented itself at a time when I had nothing better to do than take the heavy, wet clothes to the Laundromat, and this night was no exception.

So it was in this frame of mind that I was driving to the place that reminded me so much of my college days, the Midnight Mecca for the Mindless, the Boardroom for the Bored, the Way Station for the Wayward, that ever-popular gathering place for people who would rather be somewhere else—the Laundromat.

On this particular night, I was especially disgruntled. I was tired, work was waiting for me the next day, and the bench I tried to stretch out on was too hard. Besides, it was directly under a roaring ceiling fan that must have been used to preserve meat. As usual, the heat from the dryers made the fans necessary, even in winter, but I did not feel like asking for a sore throat, so I looked for another way to kill the half hour it would take for my three dryers to spin me into the next cycle, the dreaded folding phase.

As I was feeling like an especially wronged suburbanite, I am afraid I did not react very kindly to *her*, either. "She" was an obviously homeless woman whom I had noticed when I first came in. She wore a grimy stocking cap over graying blond hair. Her thin vinyl coat was yellowed and wrinkled, looking like a road map of the many miles it had covered. The dull, gray double-knit slacks had skipped many a washing, and her open-toed sandals were made at least a little warmer by the dirty, mismatched white socks she wore.

As she puttered around the place, I kept my eye on her. It was hard not to notice her. Besides her appearance, she endeared herself to me and the only other occupant with a hacking cough that sounded like your favorite FM station breaking up on the interstate as you head out of town. Add to this the fact that she regularly took a tug at a bottle of something wrapped in the traditional brown bag between puffs on a limp cigarette, and you have some idea of the very righteous indignation with which I nervously observed her.

What I saw was a constant moving about, from the bench to the vending machines, to the door, to the chair, and back again. All the while she kept muttering to herself and delivering that cough every few minutes with all the unwelcome regularity of a snooze alarm. I noticed one important thing she lacked—anything remotely connected with laundry. No basket, no hangers, and absolutely no interest, it seemed, in what was going on in those machines. It occurred to me finally that she was there just because it was a warm, dry place to be. This little scene played itself out for most of the drying time until it was after midnight and the last guest had left the ball. Now it was just Weird Wanda and me, and it felt, well, creepy.

It felt like the time when I was six years old and my mother took me to Montgomery Wards to buy material for my first-day-of-school shirt. I was excited about school starting and getting the shirt, which would be green with pencils all over it, but something ruined it for me. Two nuns in full habit were also shopping for material. As a non-Catholic, I had never seen nuns in person before, and for some reason I was at once fascinated and terrified. Why were they looking at me? Were they going to kidnap me and make me a Catholic? Were they going to make me go to some school where everybody wore uniforms instead of green shirts with pencils? I remember seeing them look at each other at one point, nodding at me, and laughing. I was sure they were saying, "Look, there's our lunch!" Later (after thankfully seeing the error of my phobia about Catholics), I realized they were probably just saying, "What a cute kid," or something similar. Anyway, I literally hid behind my mother's skirt until the ordeal was over. It was close, but we managed to get out of the store without my life-style being changed or my becoming an entree.

Now, in this dreary Laundromat, those feelings about the nuns came back. Was Wanda really something other than what she appeared to be? Not that she was hungry enough to eat me or interested at all in my conversion, but something told me not to turn my back on her. After all, she had acted suspiciously all night and now we were alone. I remained constantly aware of her position in the room as I retrieved my dry clothes and folded them.

Wanda kept up her movements, but now that it was just the two of us, she seemed more aware of me, too. Once or twice she caught me watching her and when there was a brief moment of eye contact, she appeared ready to speak.

Not really being in the mood for conversation, I was relieved that she chose not to initiate anything. I gathered the piles of warm clothes and loaded them into my two plastic baskets. The excess of this family-of-five load of laundry went into a large plastic trash bag I had also brought. I was immediately reminded of another irritation I have with this chore. The laundry, when it comes out of the dryer, is twice as large and bulky as before. I was sure that it would take two trips to get it to the car.

This realization led me to decide that I could do the impossible—carry two baskets and one trash bag full of clothes at the same time. I stacked the baskets, gathered up the top of the bag between a few fingers of my right hand, and headed for the door. I was ready to get out of this place and away from Wanda as soon as possible, even if it cost me a hernia.

As I approached the door, Wanda was about twenty feet away, near the vending machine. I felt her eyes on me as she munched her potato chips. *Almost there*, I thought, *if I can just manage the door…*

Suddenly, Wanda went wild! Here it comes, I thought. I knew it couldn't be true that I would get out of this without a scene. I had expected anything from an awkward conversation to a hard sell pitch for a handout, but an all-out frontal assault? She charged at me, yelling something made unintelligible by the potato chips tumbling from her mouth, and waving her arms in a way that made her almost drop her bottle. My pounding heart made it hard to hear my own thoughts. What had she said? Give me your wallet? Take me home with you? Which way to Waco?

All of this went through my mind in a flash, but it was when she reached me that I became aware of what she had said—something that changed my perception of the whole evening.

"Here, let me get that for you!" turned out to be her animated plea as she ran at me and the door. She squeezed her way between my baskets and the glass door and pushed it open, now the professor dismissing the freshman from her classroom.

"Good night," she said.

"Good night. Thank you," I replied, feeling much smaller than my words.

As I drove back to suburbia, I replayed the events of the evening. My guilt over having misjudged Wanda rode with me. I repented and thanked God for several things—the fact that I had a dryer that *could* break down, a car to take my laundry to another dryer, and obviously more than enough clothes for my whole family. I gained a new insight into the fact that homeless people are just that—people—people who possess the same ability to care about others that we all do, maybe even more.

There were other lessons I gleaned from this experience as I retreated home, but the feeling that kept rising to the top was gratitude, gratitude for having been allowed a seat in this late-night classroom of life. Ever since, I have seen the Laundromat differently, not so much like a waiting room, but more like a library.

Perspective

It was a bright, crisp morning. I arrived at my office with a spring in my step, still floating on the events of the last few weeks that had brought me to this cool, autumn day. Having recently become a high school guidance counselor at a large inner-city school, I literally oozed a kind of idealism that must have seemed much too sticky-sweet to many of the battle-weary colleagues I was getting to know. Still, they were patient with me and tried not to be discouraging, although sometimes I got the impression that, when they left me, they went straight to wash their hands.

On this particular day, as I unlocked the side door of my department's suite of offices, a fair amount of that idealism was smothered in a wave of a pungent aroma that was all too familiar.

Urine! I would have known that smell anywhere, but somehow never expected to find it there. A closer inspection of the doorway revealed dark, wet stains. No doubt about it, someone had confused our entrance with the local Exxon. This was incredible! How could anybody be so crude? Did they have no shame? Was this really necessary? My incredulity rambled on in my mind. This was not supposed to happen in the place where I was going to save the world.

When I had finished my mental moralizing, I went into action. I went straight for the assistant principal's office. I went to see Joe Lem.

In order to understand what happened next, one needs to know a little about Joe Lem. Joe was the kind of guy who wouldn't even take the path of least resistance if it didn't have a handrail. He was a very nice man, but he was not known for getting excited about much of anything except quitting time. He was good to have around, though, because when we had fights (and we had them often), he was excellent. He could defuse a tense situation just by his presence and he was a great mediator with irate parents. He practiced a laid-back, "don't sweat the small stuff and eyeball it when you can" type of administration. For all the criticism of his methods (or lack of them), I still think he was ultimately motivated by a sincere concern for the kids.

It was to this great problem-solver that I took my disgusting discovery, but I decided to do it indirectly. Just in case I was wrong, in case the blossoms on the bush next to the door were to blame, or some new cleaning fluid was being used, or maybe I was remembering the smell of my newborn son's diapers that morning, I didn't tell him what I had discovered. Instead, I asked him to accompany me to the scene of this monumental affront to decency, to see if he could tell what was wrong.

We stepped out the door and the fumes again hit me in the face. Full of that kind of self-importance that you feel when you know something no one else knows, I said, "Take a whiff. Do you smell anything?"

Joe drew in a deep breath, turning his head. He paused politely, then answered, "No, can't say I do. Anything wrong?"

I was crushed. I could not accept the fact that this travesty had left no impression on him. I mumbled something about it being just me and then followed him as he stepped toward the door. On his way back in, he paused and said, "Oh, by the way, they've been peein' on your door again. I'll get somebody to clean it up."

I learned a valuable lesson that day. Perspective. It's all in the way you see something, and the way you see it is colored by who you are and where you have been. Five years later, I would help Joe Lem break up a really *bad* fight. A large, muscular boy had gone to his car, taken his shirt off, come back wielding his tire jack like an axe, and had gotten his opponent on the ground. He was chopping away at the kid's head. As I pushed my way through the crowd to get to them, I remember thinking not about why someone would do such a horrible thing, but about whether the kid on the ground was going to be hurt or not, whether we would be able to calm the crowd faster than last time, and the larger issue of everybody's safety.

As it turned out, none of the blows from the makeshift axe found their mark, and ol' Joe Lem soon had things under control. At the end of the school day, the axe man, now suspended, returned to school with a gun. He took a shot at his counterpart in the parking lot and missed, then drove off. There was plenty of excitement, concern, and even laughter about the way some of our "baddest" kids had run when they heard the gunshot, but we all gave a relieved sigh that another day was over.

I never totally lost my idealism (still haven't), but I gained a better appreciation for Joe Lem that day—a new perspective, you might say. I also realized over the years since then that I had developed a marked tolerance for the smell of urine.

"What's this about an assembly today?" said the teacher. "I planned a test for today!"

It is a common conflict. Something is planned, publicized ad nauseam, and somebody still does not get the word. Very often the reply of the principal will be, "Well, it was on your weekly bulletin and on the marquee for a week, and besides, we made announcements."

Stop right there. That's the problem. Even if the written messages did not get through, administrators around the world labor under a huge misconception: that people actually listen to announcements over the public address system. As a middle school principal and assistant principal before that, I found many times that even if I was in the room observing while someone else made the routine announcements, very little in the form of listening ever takes place.

It seems that there are always more important things to do: catch up on homework, ask a terribly involved question, comb your hair, put on more makeup (after all, it's already 9:15), play paper football, flirt, sleep, you name it. Come to think of it, the *kids* don't listen either!

What to do? Many principals have tried unique ways to

get attention. Some boom into the microphone with such saccharine enthusiasm that the effect is to turn everyone even farther away (*"Good morning, students! This is another thinly veiled attempt by a middle-aged adult to be cool."*). I knew one high school principal several years ago who actually had a set of chimes next to the microphone, on which he played "Reveille," the Army wake-up tune, every morning to whet the pallet for such morsels as "The Public Law Form 874 that has been distributed is for students whose parents work on federal property only..." The problem, besides the need for more interesting material, was that he could not play the chimes very *well,* so the audience, if there was one, was always about five notes ahead of him on the song. By the time he got through the entire thing, we all were on our second cup of coffee and the entertainment was over. He had lost us.

Another principal I knew made it a point to mention every day at the end of the announcements some profound words of wisdom from some great source. It was all well intentioned, meant to inspire. Then he would always end it with, "have a good day—or *not.* The choice is up to you!" That ought to get them.

Wrong. By the time they had heard it a few times, they began to anticipate it, and all over the room you could see sixth-graders doing their best lip-synch impression of the principal. There has to be a better way.

There is. It is not an obvious approach, however. It takes a little deception and some creativity. It is what I call the "bogus announcement."

After years of making announcements as an assistant principal and finding that no one heard them, I developed the theory that there was one simple reason for that. They were *boring*. It seemed that if plugging the bake sale for the local boy scouts was not exactly "The Simpsons," then we had to insert some material here and there that, though not factual in any way, people might notice just for its absurdity, if nothing else. At least someone may hear about the assembly coming up, even if just by accident. So, I began to use my imagination to create some originals and adapted a few jokes to come up with some zingers that I thought might at least get people to say, "Hey! Did he mean to say that?" The following announcements are based on jokes I heard from other sources, so even though their sources are unknown, they should get some of the credit:

1. Due to the enormous volume of mail handled during the Christmas rush, the Post office is asking you, in order to save time, to please break your own packages this year before mailing them.

2. If Mrs. Reese looks a little confused today about what period it is, it's because she put instant coffee in the microwave and went *back* in time!

3. If Mr. Contreras looks confused today, it's because he got a bump on the head and is having amnesia and déjà vu at the same time, so now he forgets everything *twice*.

4. Teachers: there will be an organizational meeting after school next week for those of you who are interested in forming a parent group to study reading problems. The name of the organization is D.A.M.—"Mothers Against Dyslexia."

5. Students: the guidance department would like us to announce that as you think about choosing colleges, you should be aware that Texas A&M University has disbanded its water polo team. Too many horses were drowning.

6. Students: we are very sorry to have to announce that the surprise musical assembly we had planned for you today has been canceled. We had arranged for country singer Willie Nelson to make an appearance at our school, but we are told he cannot come because he is in the hospital after being hit by a truck last night. It seems he was out playing "On the Road Again."

7. (First week of school) Teachers: if you have students on your class roll that are withdrawn, send them to the counselor. Maybe she can bring them out of their shells.

8. Students: most of you are making a good effort to do well in your classes. We want to take time to thank you for trying. We know that you are trying because your teachers tell us that some of you are the most trying students they have ever had!

9. Please be on the lookout around the campus for an angry, stray, orphaned, three-legged dog. He is looking for the dogcatcher who took his paw!

Then came the challenge of making them up totally from scratch, or from some idea based on something that had happened, but had not been formally written as a "joke." If the humor in these (should you find any) seems more adult than middle school students could usually be expected to get, don't forget that much of it was meant to reach the teachers because they're not listening either. Besides, I was often surprised to find that many students understood the subtleties quite well. Here are a few:

1. *Teachers:* there will be a workshop soon for those of you who are members of the National Association of Psychics … you'll know when and where …

2. *(Second day of school) Teachers:* we are trying to get an accurate count of our enrollment for the central office. Please tell your students that if they were here yesterday but are not here today, they should raise their hands.

3. *Students:* the track team is in need of a volunteer to help them out. If any of you sixth-graders are interested in being a javelin catcher, please see the coach …

4. *(End of year) Students:* please remember that any of you who fail Redundancy will have to repeat it.

5. The social studies department would like to invite you to hear a famous guest speaker. He is a Japanese veteran of World War II who flew over 500 Kamikaze missions. His name is No Die Yet and he will speak on "Last-minute Decision Making."

6. *Students:* those of you who are absent on the 31st will have to make up your work on the 32nd …

7. *Teachers:* we have a very important announcement for you from the National Organization for the Reduction of Paperwork. Unfortunately, we can't find it in the pile on my desk.

8. Today is the anniversary of the passage of an important piece of legislation on gun control, which prohibits the possession of a handgun without certain security checks. It is called the Brady Law, not to be confused with the Brady Bunch Law, which prohibits the creation of precocious stepfamilies.

9. The post-election support group for people who did not vote at all in last week's mayor's race because all of the choices were too depressing will meet Saturday at 1:00 … in Memorial Stadium.

10. *Students:* listen carefully to the following announcement. I will give a dollar to the first student who can tell me how many times the word "school" is NOT mentioned in this announcement.

11. If you have found a bladeless knife without any handles, please return it to the kitchen.

12. (We had a secretary whose name was Dolly Burk.) *Thought for the Day:* If Mrs. Burk went to South America on one of those mountain hiking and camping trips and they gave her one of those funny-looking pack animals to carry all of her stuff, would that animal be known as the "Dolly Llama"?

13. The following students need to come by the office to pick up their Perfect Attendance Awards, due to being absent on the day of the assembly.

The most common reaction I would get from these announcements was a groan or a chuckle from a teacher, or a question from a student, who might say, "Was that real?"

or something like that. At least I knew they had listened. I did have a student once who came in and said she knew the answer to the riddle about how many times "school" was not mentioned. She guessed "infinity," and I had to give her the dollar. I should have given her ten for proving my point—that it does make them listen and that they can also *think*. I felt sorry, however, for the poor little guy who came up to me after the javelin-catcher plug and asked how to go about signing up. I don't think he appreciated finding out it was bogus.

There have been other times, too, when students' gullibility has shown they are no match for the PA. Once, when a calculator was stolen from the cafeteria and was not reported to the office until five minutes before the end of the day, I decided something needed to be done. You cannot let the sun set on stolen goods in the school business or you are likely never to see them again. I got on the PA and said, "We have had a very valuable Casio calculator stolen from the cafeteria. It had been treated with a special invisible ink so that, if you are in contact with it too long, it will turn your hands green. If you see this calculator anywhere, please turn it in." There was a kid at my secretary's desk in 60 seconds with the calculator, claiming he "found" it.

Another time, the assistant principal at the elementary school next door to the middle school where I was an assistant called me and said they had had a bike stolen from their rack (possibly by one of my students) and asked if I would try to find it. The next day, a bike matching the description of the stolen one was found by a custodian just outside our back door, early in the morning before kids started arriving. Knowing we had the right bike, but not having the perpetrator yet, I decided to try something. As soon as school started, I got on the horn and said, "Early this morning a bike was found outside our door. If you are missing a bike and can accurately describe this one, please see me..." Within minutes a kid named Cory showed up to claim the bike, describing it perfectly, although we and the police had already identified the elementary-aged owner. Apparently, Cory had thought that since we appeared to think the bike was just lost, we would not know that he had stolen it and abandoned it there. Once again the PA came in handy and it was actually *heard.*

We have found truant kids sometimes by using this tool, also. If someone ends up missing from a class, we search for a little while, and then we pick up the microphone. A simple "Butch Jenkins, please report to the office to pick up your reward money," or "...your ride is here," gets them almost every time.

Sometimes the fun backfires, however. It pays for whoever is making the announcements to proof them first and to spend a little time in general preparation before reading them. It pays, but I almost never did it. One day, in a rush and typically ill-prepared, I picked up the microphone to make the daily second period announcements. People with panicked looks on their faces started running in and out of the room and handing me little blurbs for this or that thing that they had hurriedly scrawled on bits of paper. I frowned at them as I kept reading. How could they be even less prepared than I? Then a girls' coach handed me a little yellow sticky note and fled the room. Irritated, I read it into the microphone, "It's only *first* period, dummy!" I looked up and saw the coach at the door laughing, with all the office staff joining in behind her. I could only imagine what was happening in the classrooms.

The PA is a powerful thing. It can bring good or evil into the life of a school. It is like having a voice that can reach a thousand souls at once, or it can simply annoy the adolescent spirits and, at best, fall victim to their apathy. It is limited only by the creativity of the announcer.

Now hear this! Now hear this! Students! If you are one of those people who hates to draw attention to yourself in a group, would you please stand ...

Every assistant principal struggles with the same thing. How do you settle an argument when you have witnessed neither its beginning nor its cause? When adolescents argue, they do not listen to adult reasoning any better than they listen to announcements. They become unaware that anyone else is anywhere on the planet. All that matters is winning the point. The idea is to wear down your opponent to the point that he may even *agree* with you, just to end the fight! This logic could almost always be applied to favorite teams, presidential candidates, or prettiest girls, but not to basketballs.

To an adolescent boy, a basketball is a sacred thing. It is his connection to the dream world of the NBA, where everybody is bigger and richer than both of his parents. It is his *baby*. It is his companion on the playground when no one else is there and his bargaining chip when his is the only ball there. It goes with him to his room, rolls around under his feet in the car, and gets on his mother's last nerve when it bounces too often on the living room floor. My wife and I even had to take one away from our son many times on the way into *church*. Let's face it—when you are thirteen, your basketball is your bud and until it dies on the neighbor's thorn bush, or breathes its last on a rusty nail, or simply fades away from neglect in the corner of the backyard because you got a new indoor-outdoor Wilson, it will never let you down.

Knowing this made my dilemma that much greater when I encountered Jay and Eddie after school one day in the midst of their argument. Instead of arguing about baseball cards, video games, or even girls, they had engaged in combat over a life-or-death matter—the ownership of a well-worn orange rubber basketball.

"What's the problem?" I asked.

"He's got my ball!" said Jay.

"No, I don't," countered Eddie. "It's *my* ball!"

"No way, man, I left it here for a while and you stole it!" Jay yelled. He went on to show certain marks on the ball that he said he recognized, which were proof to him of his ownership, but did not do me much good.

They went back and forth on this for a while and I could not interject. All the time I was thinking, "How could this be? They can't both be right. Maybe they could both be *wrong* and the ball doesn't really belong to either one, but they can't both be *right.*"

This situation called for wisdom. Who was the wisest person I knew? Certainly not me, or even anyone close to me. It had to be King Solomon, who at a young age was given the choice of whatever gift he wanted. He had already been wise enough to choose wisdom over riches or fame and when his wish was granted, the latter came to him also.

Anyway, I had grown up with the Biblical account of Solomon holding court (1 Kings 3:16–28). The story says that two prostitutes who lived together were brought to him locked in mortal combat over the ownership of a baby. It seems that the two had given birth to their offspring within a few days of each other and one night as they slept with their newborns at their sides, one woman rolled over and accidentally smothered her baby, so that she awoke in the night to find him dead. Her roommate, the second woman, claimed that the first had switched her dead baby with the live one while the second woman slept, so that she would think her baby was the one that had died. In the morning light, this woman knew better, and thus the argument.

Solomon had considered this for a while, then made a surprising command. Asking for a sword to be brought to him, he proposed to cut the living baby in half and give each woman a half, to be fair. Immediately one of the women, out of compassion for her son, begged the king not to cut the child in half, but to give him to the other woman so that he could live. Wise Solomon then knew that she was the mother, because she so quickly thought not of herself but of the son she loved. She was awarded the baby.

Hmmmm, I thought. Could I use this now in some small way? I decided a literal application would not work, because it was too abstract for these little guys to grasp, and if I had suggested cutting the ball in half, they would both think I was crazy. But a little twist on Solomon's tactics might help, I thought. Anyway, I had no better ideas and the constant whining of these two was about to wear me down.

"Hold on, you guys. I've got an idea. How about sharing the ball? Jay, you can use it on Mondays, Wednesdays, and

Fridays, and Eddie, you can have it on Tuesdays, Thursdays, and Saturdays. On Sundays, nobody will use it. Okay?"

For a split second I had a terrible fear that they might actually go for this arrangement, and *I* would be the one stuck with enforcing it, but then they came through with their true colors.

"That's okay with me," said Eddie.

"No way, man!" protested Jay, the tears flowing freely now. "Why would I want to share my ball with him?"

I looked at Jay and saw the connection between him and that beat-up old orange companion of his.

"Take your ball and go home, Jay," I said. "And put your *name* on it! And Eddie, you come to my office and let's talk about respecting other people's property…"

Neither one argued with that.

As far as I know, Solomon was never an assistant princi-pal. If he had been, however, he probably would have come up with a better way to solve the problem. But I do know that his wisdom continues to be passed down and even when it is somewhat twisted, it *works*.

Joey Makes the Call

Having a pay phone in a school can be what is called an *attractive nuisance*. It is something you want for its convenience, but it will almost always cause problems. Still, the general public, and particularly parents, tend to take it for granted that in a place as public as a school, there will always be one around.

The problem with pay phones in schools, however, is that kids never seem to have any money. The same kid you saw buying fourteen chocolate chip cookies at lunch will not have two quarters to his name at 5:00 when his detention is over and he needs to call his mom, whom he forgot to tell about his detention and who will any moment be calling the National Guard because she could not get him at home at the customary 4:30 check-in time when the bus drops him off. So, he is at the door of the office, begging, "Can I please use the office phone?" (Something that is officially forbidden but unofficially allowed, so as not to have too many kids standing around at 6:00 waiting to be picked up by a frantic parent or a company of National Guardsmen.)

"What's the matter with the pay phone? Why don't you use it?" is usually my response.

"I don't got no money," the kid says.

"'I don't have any money,'" I correct him, in my best teacher tone.

"You don't got none, neither?" he replies.

Never mind. I let him in and he calls Mom, just before the jeeps roll. It happens so often, but the bottom line is, the pay phone has to stay.

It was the existence of such pay phones that proved to be too much temptation for Joey, a cute little sixth-grader who decided to pull a very unoriginal prank—a bogus 911 call. Such false alarms are technically illegal and we warn kids constantly about this, but still they manage to make them sometimes. The fact is they are extremely hard to catch when they do it, and they know it.

So it happened that one day we had the latest in a string of these phony calls during a routine morning. The police showed up, as usual, and were in their customary foul mood when they found it was a fake, as suspected. We assured them we would try to find the culprit, but we all knew that was usually an exercise in futility. My assistant principal for sixth grade, Terry, made an attempt to get some information, but there was really none to get.

As the morning wore on, however, things began to develop. An announcement was made asking for information and gradually a few students trickled into the office to offer names. The one name that kept coming up, however, was Joey. What made it interesting to Terry was that the reason they had Joey's name was not because anybody *saw* him make the call. It was because he was *bragging* that he made the call. When Terry called Joey in to interrogate him, he put on his best poker face and denied everything. Everybody else, he now said, was lying. He did not say he did it. Then, as it often turns out, his story changed.

There is something about adolescent lying that has always intrigued me. I have found, and Terry had too, that if you ask the kid to repeat the story, he can never do it the same way again if it is a lie. So, as Terry had Joey repeat his story several times, it was not surprising that it evolved into an admission that he said it, but he was "only kidding."

As I was walking by Terry's office about this time, my frustrated assistant called me in with them. "Joey here has been bragging that he made the 911 call this morning and now he claims he was just kidding, but he has told half the school and he lied to me about it at first, so I think he did it, but maybe you would like to ask him about it."

Joey was nervous as I sat down next to him. He squirmed in his chair like a baby who wants out of a lap. I tried a line of questioning like Terry's and got the same result. "I was just kidding. I didn't do it," was his insistent, agitated defense.

Fearing it would not work, I nevertheless decided I would try something anyway, for lack of a better idea. As soon as I asked the question, I suspected that he did not understand it, but little did I know that it would have the result that it did.

My doubt grew out of my forgetting that adolescents do not grasp abstract concepts all that well. They are not as sophisticated as we adults (or most of us) are, when it comes to accepting a premise that is not necessarily true, just for the sake of argument. The ordinary syllogism that says that a certain characteristic of all of set A is true, B is a subset of A, therefore the conclusion (C) that B possesses that characteristic has to be true. Does that make sense? An example I heard long ago went something like this:

A. All three-legged snakes are green.

B. Johnny has a three-legged snake.

C. Johnny's snake is green.

To us as adults, this makes sense. But to an adolescent, the first thing he is going to say, and with good reason, is, "That's stupid. Snakes don't have legs!" We adults can suspend our perception of reality long enough to listen and follow the argument. Not so with sixth-graders, who have to have things explained in a very literal way. That is why they do not get subtle adult humor. It has to be visually funny, or otherwise very concrete in its meaning, until the sense of humor has had enough experience to anticipate the absurdity that makes good humor.

Completely ignoring all of this, I plunged into my hypothetical question for Joey that, halfway through, I was sure was a waste of time. I said, "Joey, this doesn't make any sense. If someone was breaking into houses in your neighborhood and the police were asking around to see who might have done it, you wouldn't be telling people you did it if you really didn't, would you?"

Thinking that made perfect sense to me, but figuring I had lost him after "Joey," I was completely caught off guard by his response.

His eyes widening as he heard "breaking in" and "police," Joey exclaimed, "Now look, I *did* the 911 call, but I didn't break into *nobody's* house!"

Thank you, Joey. You're suspended.

Roma, the Lesbian Gang Girl

I first met Roma when she was in the seventh grade. Her attitude matched her name. It was a feminine name with a kind of a macho roll to it. That was Roma.

The year was about 1981. This smooth-featured, dark-eyed Hispanic adolescent was wearing a red bandana around her head, over her short, straight black hair, a t-shirt under a sleeveless U.S. Army fatigue jacket, and leather straps around her wrists. Fake tattoos frequently covered her coffee-colored shoulders. As her school counselor, I got to know her very quickly after she transferred into our large city middle school, joining our already large share of tough characters.

Roma liked to fight. It did not make much difference to her what the issue was or even who was fighting. To her it always proved something.

This penchant for pugilism made Roma an easy target for La Familia, a gang that had just formed in the community and at our school. Its main leaders, we thought, were at another nearby middle school and at the high school where our kids matriculated. The group's main theme was female camaraderie taken to the extreme, and they called themselves, quite proudly, a "lesbian" gang. It was not that adopting a lesbian lifestyle was necessarily a prerequisite for membership. It was just that the image was there and if you got in, you got in. No one outside the group knew for certain much more than that. Gangs, however, are more about acceptance and belonging than about sexual preference.

At any rate, Roma told me how she felt that, in La Familia, she had found herself. The boys had not flirted with her (they were terrified of her) and the popular girls had shunned her tomboy get-up and masculine mannerisms, as well as her love of fighting. Here in the gang, there were no pretenses. You could be the type of female you wanted to be and everybody else had better leave you alone, which they did.

Thus, Roma and friends pretty much ruled the playground…until the skating rink thing happened. People talked about it for months, how La Familia had been in full force at the skating rink one night, how a hapless black boy had challenged them, and how he was stabbed to death by at least one of the girls. The incident was the beginning of the end for Roma.

Although the law never really pointed the finger at Roma, she had been there and she grew quieter daily about the glories of La Familia. School and grades were already pretty hopeless and now legal problems from the skating rink thing loomed ahead. A common answer for parents with kids in this kind of trouble, even when there are no crimes involved, is to move. Some adult in Roma's life made the decision that a change in her environment (in this case from Texas to Michigan) would be good for her. With the successful completion of her eighth-grade year in serious jeopardy, off she went, and I guessed I would never see her again.

We have a saying in this business that goes something like, "When a kid who has been causing trouble for everyone else moves away, don't celebrate the loss of a problem, get ready for another problem to move in." That is the way it works. People in trouble with limited solutions move to greener pastures, higher ground, something new. It's human nature.

About a year after Roma left, I changed jobs. I transferred voluntarily to one of the roughest high schools in town because I wanted to see if I could make some difference there. I thought, after five years as a middle school counselor, I could now conquer the high school world. I became the freshman counselor and I was myself a freshman in another sense of the word.

One day in mid-year I was given the task of registering a new student. This was a routine part of my job and many of these new students did not leave much of an impression. But this one was different. Physically, she was unforgettable. She wore a tight vinyl skirt that barely reached to mid-thigh over black stockings. The skirt was a metallic green that was hard to ignore. Her sleeveless blouse was a bright orange. Together with the skirt, it framed a very feminine figure underneath. There were lots of gaudy accessories—bracelets, earrings, chains—and a pair of high heels that had probably never seen a school. The hair was short, but wavy and very feminine. This image was made complete by an eye makeup job that any televangelist's wife would have coveted openly.

Interestingly, I think it was in those eyes that I saw something familiar. Without looking at the name on the card, I knew it was Roma. My ego and my usual optimism about saving the world took a little dive when it became apparent that Roma did not remember me, at least at first. We renewed our acquaintance however and were able to establish a little rapport before she wiggled her shiny skirt into her new classes.

After Roma left my office, I reflected on all that had happened to her, only a little more than a year earlier and what must have happened since. Someone else had been convicted of the stabbing at the skating rink, so her legal problems were apparently over. She had moved away and had apparently gotten some kind of counseling in Michigan, whether formally or from friends and family, and now was coming back home. She was now on the other side of town, in high school instead of middle school, and ready to try life from a different angle.

Unfortunately, the new approach presented some new problems. Roma began to date. Every metallic skirt-chaser in the school lined up for a chance. Roma, the "reformed" lesbian, fell in love with one of them, a "hunk" named Rudy. Rudy already had a steady girlfriend named Andrea, but the mystique that Roma had created with her striking (if not overdone) appearance was too much for him. Unable to resist her attentions, Rudy got Roma pregnant within a couple of months of her triumphant return to the heterosexual world.

Now what? Rudy did the only thing he felt he could do. I tried to get him to stay in school, but at sixteen he dropped out and married Roma, all the time agonizing over the loss of Andrea, his beautiful girlfriend.

As for Andrea, she spent the next few weeks crying over the episode. Not realizing, as we so-called sensible adults did, that in many ways she was extremely fortunate to have been spared Roma's plight, she repeatedly wept all over my desk about the fact that she wished Rudy had gotten *her* pregnant, instead. Of course she would say that. Such is the reasoning of a sixteen-year-old in love.

I lost track of all of these teenagers, so I don't now who stayed with whom, or what became of the baby or the marriage. I hope they all made it. I hope Andrea got over it and counted her blessings. I hope Rudy got a job and felt good about the sacrifice he made. And, I hope Roma found herself again and this time it was less painful. She deserved that.

One of the best jobs I ever had was that of a high school guidance counselor. I guess one reason I loved it was the view of life it gave me. I saw all kinds of humanity come through my office, and like all counselors, I often tried to change it. But mostly I just marveled at the variety of the species.

The most tedious duty in this job was building a schedule for new students when they arrived. One day, that task became much more interesting, as a strange coincidence brought two new students to my office at the same time from the same distant part of the world—Los Angeles, California. *East* Los Angeles, at that. How these two strangers ended up moving to Austin, Texas on the same day, I never knew.

The first was a boy. He was a tall, African-American sixteen-year-old, whose speech was cluttered with slang and he had a definite street-wise look. In conversation, however, he seemed to have more of the "wanna be" kind of attitude than a genuine toughness. When we had completed the scheduling chore, I said, "Tell me about East Los Angeles. Is it really as bad as they say?"

"It a lot worse!" he said, showing obvious relief at having left there. "In fact, it terrible. If you walk down da street wit a red rag in yo pocket, da blue rag gang come ovah and beat you up. If you walk down da street wit a blue rag in yo pocket, da red rag gang come ovah and beat you up. It a bad place to be, man. Not safe for nobody." His vernacular was a testimony to his self-assumed street wisdom.

We chatted a little more, then I sent him on to his new classes, wondering what kind of day he was going to have, especially since many people felt our own inner-city high school was itself not exactly a sanctuary for beleaguered pedestrians.

Next up was a girl, also African-American, also from East LA, and, like the boy, appearing to be very street-wise. She had been waiting in the outer office and had not heard my conversation with the first student. We struggled through the registration routine and then I decided to get another opinion.

"Do you know that guy who just left here?" I asked. "He's from your neighborhood, apparently…"

"Nope. Never seen him," she said in a voice not cluttered with slang.

We commented on their coincidental arrival at our school, then I said, "He says it's pretty rough out there in LA—gangs, violence, crime, and all that. Says hc is really glad to be out of there. How do you feel about it?"

"It's not so bad," she smiled without hesitation. She seemed even a little homesick for the place. "One thing I know, though, is you don't *ever* walk down the street with a *rag* in your pocket!"

Participant or victim. Which do we want to be? We all choose, regardless of the surroundings, which of these roles we want to take. And it *is* a choice.

It was going to be a good day at our school for that new

girl. She would be a little lost, she would be late for a class or two, but she would meet a new friend who was late too. She would participate, she would not be a victim, and she would survive.

And, if I remember correctly, the boy was in a fight by *lunchtime.*

Zenobia & the Rainstorm

Zenobia was thirteen years old and weighed three hundred pounds. She was one of those kids you would have talked to about low self-esteem, if she had suffered from it. The problem was, Zenobia's weight was a problem to everybody but *her*.

I was Zenobia's counselor in a public junior high school of about one thousand students, where she was a seventh-grader. Her parents had been consulted. The nurse alternated between compassion and diet books, but nothing seemed to affect her resolve to be the way she was. Her peers either looked to her for protection against others, avoided her out of fear for their own safety, or watched her, bemused, from afar like some kind of colossal oddity.

It was intcresting to watch Zenobia get around. Physically, she handled the task with no real difficulty, but she had a hard time remaining inconspicuous. Her size made other people wince sympathetically, but they soon realized they did not need to. Zenobia was just *big* and she did not mind who knew it. She reminded me of the college professor I had who weighed about 350 pounds. When someone asked him how, with so much bulk, he managed to get around, he answered, "I generally make two trips!"

Had Zenobia possessed his age and wit, she would haves answered like that. As it was, to be kind, she was too young to be that sophisticated and wit was not her strong suit. She dealt with her weight by two methods: ignore or intimidate. The latter seemed to work with most students. She may have known that they sometimes laughed at her, but she didn't show it and heaven help the poor kids who laughed at her too long or too loud. All of this resulted in Zenobia's acquiring a reputation. The word was out that the girl was just plain *mean*.

So it came to pass that one day Zenobia went to the bus stop in the morning and got caught in an early spring downpour. There was no cover at the stop and she had to stand there for a good ten minutes before the bus showed up. Now, this was no light shower. It was not even what you call a heavy rain. This was no oops-teacher-my-dress-is-a-little-soggy-may-I-have-a-towel-please kind of accident. This was a good ol' gully-washin', ankle-dippin,' shoe-squeakin,' roof-leakin' Texas rainstorm, the kind that could float bricks. By the time Zenobia finally got to school, this girl and her huge, tent-like flowered dress could have registered on their own rain gauge.

If Zenobia's bus had been on time, what happened next might never have transpired, but it was late, delayed by the storm. She arrived at school just before the bell rang for her first class. She raised a few eyebrows and made a lot of noise as she squished through the halls, but most people did not notice. Most of them were not exactly dry as toast, either.

Zenobia's first-period class was in a portable classroom that was joined to another by a small foyer. Instead of sloshing on in with the other overexcited students (rain makes them act even more like junior high kids), she paused in the foyer. A few minutes went by before the teacher missed the girl and stepped out to check on her. When she opened the door, there it was—the scene of the year. Zenobia was standing patiently in the middle of the foyer, *minus* her dress. She was magnificent in her huge, white bra and an equally spacious white half-slip. There, draped over the top of an open door, was her gigantic, flowered dress, still dribbling into a gathering pool on the floor.

At this point, the only thing larger than the teacher's gaping mouth might have been the eyeballs of the students now filling up the doorway behind her. Across the foyer, the other class had also emerged to check on the fuss outside their room. Zenobia met their stares with eyes that showed all the concern of a bored housewife at the Laundromat.

"I ain't about to wear that nasty wet dress to class!" she declared. "I'm stayin' right here 'til it's dry."

It was not until later that the teacher who related this incident realized the full impact of it. It was, she said, the first time that the other students had been forced to confront Zenobia and her hulking frame head-on *and no one had laughed!* Instead, there was a quiet, awkward moment and then business as usual. Students went back to their seats, she went back to waiting, and the dress went back to drying.

This day was a landmark for Zenobia. Who knows what this lovable but surly girl had intended, but somehow she had managed to get her peers to face (literally) what it was about her that was so offensive and to realize, one way or the other, that it was, pardon the pun, *no big deal.*

From then on, kids treated Zenobia differently. They seemed

to accept her more like a member of the family you had seen
walking around the house in their underwear when you knew
there was a very good reason for it—*no big deal.* Maybe it was
her own realization that she was part of some kind of "family" at
the school, or a natural maturing process, or just a clear sky and
a dry dress, but after that rainstorm, Zenobia started to treat
those kids, and herself, a little differently, too.

Epilogue

So the journey continues to Zenobia and beyond, charted by the landmark lessons learned along the way. There will always be paper and pencil, computers and videos, and piles and piles of tests. But the element that is a constant in all of education is made up of students, teachers, administrators, counselors, librarians, nurses, teacher aides, office workers, parent-teacher organizations, soccer moms, working parents, and stay-at-home parents—the *human* element. Its molecules make up a universal garment we wear, whether in the form of a green pencil shirt or a dripping floral dress.

Robert Fulgham says, "We are the only creatures that both laugh and weep. I think it's because we are the only creatures that can see the difference between the way things are and the way they might be." [1] I believe God intended it that way and there is no place where this is truer than in schools. May your children and your grandchildren's children continue their journeys, live their stories, remember them, and share them with others. It's what keeps us all human.

Endnotes

1. Robert Fulgham, *It Was On Fire When I Lay Down On It.* (New York: Villard Books, 1988), p. 218.

listen|imagine|view|experience

AUDIO BOOK DOWNLOAD INCLUDED WITH THIS BOOK!

In your hands you hold a complete digital entertainment package. Besides purchasing the paper version of this book, this book includes a free download of the audio version of this book. Simply use the code listed below when visiting our website. Once downloaded to your computer, you can listen to the book through your computer's speakers, burn it to an audio CD or save the file to your portable music device (such as Apple's popular iPod) and listen on the go!

How to get your free audio book digital download:

1. Visit www.tatepublishing.com and click on the e|LIVE logo on the home page.
2. Enter the following coupon code:
   0db2-1594-02f8-94d0-7400-fc34-689a-8efa
3. Download the audio book from your e|LIVE digital locker and begin enjoying your new digital entertainment package today!